Lateral MINDTRAP®

Puzzles

Challenge the way you think & see

DETECTIVE SHADOW

PUZZLE WRIGHT PRESS

An imprint of Sterling Publishing Co., Inc.

www.puzzlewright.com

Puzzlewright Press and the distinctive Puzzlewright Press logo are registered trademarks of Sterling Publishing Co., Inc.

Library of Congress Cataloging-in-Publication Data Available

15   17   19   20   18   16

Distributed in Canada by Sterling Publishing
$^c/o$ Canadian Manda Group, 165 Dufferin Street
Toronto, Ontario, Canada M6K 3H6
Distributed in the United Kingdom by GMC Distribution Services
Castle Place, 166 High Street, Lewes, East Sussex, England BN7 1XU
Distributed in Australia by Capricorn Link (Australia) Pty. Ltd.
P.O. Box 704, Windsor, NSW 2756, Australia

Printed in China
Sterling ISBN 978-0–8069–7135–3

For information about custom editions, special sales, premium and corporate purchases, please contact Sterling Special Sales Department at 800-805-5489 or specialsales@sterlingpublishing.com.

If you enjoy this book, please look for Detective Shadow's book, *Tricky MindTrap® Puzzles*, by Puzzlewright Press, which includes brainteasers, trick questions, and optical illusions. These MindTrap® puzzle books, like the game on which they are based, will capture your imagination and challenge the way you think and see.

Lateral MindTrap® Contents

◆ "I wouldn't want this musty old dump if you gave it to me," snapped Ida Gamble. "Look," replied Sam Sham, "Clem may have been a whacked-out hermit, but I have a feeling he hid a fortune on this property. This house has been boarded up for 7 years. All you need to do is pay the back taxes and, er, my modest fee, and this little gem is all yours!" "I'm outta here!" cried Ida. "Wait, just let me show you the secret staircase I found." Sam pulled back the oakpress paper paneling to reveal the hidden staircase. "Look, that step is loose, and there's something shiny behind it!" Sam pulled back the loose step to discover a small collection of shiny sterling silver cutlery. "I knew it!" exclaimed Sam, "This house contains a fortune! I think I'll buy it myself." "Not so fast," replied Ida, "you offered me the house and I just bought it." How do you know that Ida has just been scammed?

◆ Sid Shady was waving frantically as Shadow pulled up to his oceanfront home. "Hurry!" shouted Shady. "My wife's been murdered!" Shadow opened the bedroom door and surveyed the gruesome scene. Mrs. Shady lay dead on the floor, a knife planted in her back. The smell of a recently extinguished candle permeated the air. A puddle of water and a broken jug lay near her head. As always at this time of night, a light breeze blew off the ocean through the open window. Shadow crossed the room, pulled the window shut and turned to face Shady. "I was downstairs when I heard a loud crash and a scream," began Shady. "I raced upstairs to find my wife lying on the floor. Rather than touch anything, I immediately called the police." "That's a lie!" replied Shadow. Why would he say that?

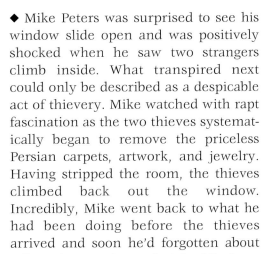

◆ Mike Peters was surprised to see his window slide open and was positively shocked when he saw two strangers climb inside. What transpired next could only be described as a despicable act of thievery. Mike watched with rapt fascination as the two thieves systematically began to remove the priceless Persian carpets, artwork, and jewelry. Having stripped the room, the thieves climbed back out the window. Incredibly, Mike went back to what he had been doing before the thieves arrived and soon he'd forgotten about the entire incident. Why wouldn't Mike, who was in perfect health, have tried to stop the thieves, or at the very least, called the police after they had left?

◆ "I have the only key to the room containing the jewelry of my late Aunt Maggy," said Sid Shady. "Since her death a week ago, neither I nor anybody else has entered this room. I was quite pleased to hear that all her jewelry was to be sold and the proceeds to go to charity," continued Shady as he stepped around a large plant on his way to the safe. While Shady was spinning the combination lock, Shadow crossed the room to sit on the ledge of the large bay window. Shady opened the safe and removed the bag of jewels. "I'm sure these jewels of Aunt Maggy's will fetch a fortune for charity," said a smiling Sid Shady. "I'll bet these jewels are either fake or there are a few missing," replied Shadow. What made him suspicious?

◆ Art Bragg caught Charles Pompuss in the lobby of the Soul-Ace Hotel and recounted his latest adventure. "While cutting through the heavy Amazon growth, I suddenly looked up into the business end of a 6-foot (0.9-m) long blowgun with a painted savage on the other end. Soon after I'm bound hand and foot to a stake. Having studied the famous Harry Houdini, I managed to free myself and make a run for it. One of the savages saw me and gave chase. I hid behind a tree and ambushed him. I knocked him silly, took his blowgun, and headed for the river. Hearing the rest of the tribe coming, I jumped into the river and hid underwater. I must have stayed underwater for close to an hour, breathing through the blowgun. When I felt it was safe, I followed the river back to civilization." "I hope you don't expect anyone to believe that yarn," retorted Charles Pompuss. Why isn't Art's story believable?

◆ It seemed just yesterday he had taught his wife gymnastics in high school, Sid Shady thought. Today, however, it was free climbing. Suddenly Sid couldn't believe his good luck. His wife had inexplicably succumbed to an animal-like fear of heights and stood frozen against the rock. Seizing his chance and aware of spectators below, Shady began coaxing his wife to obey his commands. Gradually she turned around and put her back against the rock. Shady knew she would do what he said out of blind obedience and sheer terror. Sid drove a piton into the rock and secured the line. He knotted a safety clip to the other end and threw it to his wife's feet. Sid then instructed her to bend over and pick up the clip while being careful not to move her feet or bend her knees. As soon as she began to do so, she suddenly plunged to her death. When Shadow heard the details, he had Shady arrested. Why?

◆ Dee Septor, the world-famous magician, claimed that he was able to defy the pull of gravity. Dee claimed he could drop a small unfolded sheet of newsprint and a deck of playing cards at the same time and from the same height, and both would fall at exactly the same speed. How could he do it?

◆ Professor Quantum had purchased an old Scottish castle that was in desperate need of repair. One of his first priorities was to have the tunnel leading to the antiques storage room in the cellar wired. Luigi, the electrician, had just finished the basement wiring but had failed to label which of the three switches belonged to the storage room. Quantum had a small flashlight that would enable him to find the storage room; however, he didn't like the thought of returning for a small item armed with only a small light. Knowing

he would be back, Quantum wanted to be certain he could correctly label which switch belonged to the storage room with only one trip. How did he do it?

◆ "You've never looked lovelier," snarled Sam Sham to his wife Sadie as she attempted to wrestle her hair into submission. "Fortunately the play doesn't start for another 30 minutes and unfortunately it's a 40-minute drive," continued Sam. The Shams were going to the Broadway hit *Till Death Do Us Part*. Sam and Sadie drove around the theater twice before finding a parking spot. By this time Sam was livid. Being late, they were let in the side door and directed to their places in the darkened theater. Less than 15 minutes into the play, as if Sam had completely lost control, he slipped a nylon rope around Sadie's neck and began strangling her. She put up a fierce but silent struggle as Sam pulled the cord tighter and tighter until she finally slumped to the floor. Although the theatre was full and many people were horrified by Sam's actions, nobody dared to interfere. Why not?

◆ It happened in Alaska during the winter of 1993 when a small, fully loaded passenger plane tried to approached the runway during a violent snowstorm. The control tower regretfully informed the pilot that due to the inclement weather, the runways were closed to all air traffic. Furthermore, all airports within a 300-mile radius were also closed. Upon hearing this, the pilot immediately informed the passengers of the news while turning the plane around and heading back from where they had just come. Incredibly enough, within a half hour all the passengers were safely inside an airport terminal building. How was this possible?

◆ It was the same routine every Friday. "Hi, Sam, how's business?" inquired Barney Dribble. "Dead," replied Sam. Barney thanked Sam as they each got on their bikes and rode away. It was the last time anyone saw Barney alive. Shadow arrived on the scene to see Constable Bumlinger giving orders. "Okay, Bumlinger, what do we got?" "It's obvious, Shadow," replied Bumlinger with disdain, "It's a hit-and-run. Ya see, car hits bike, bike falls down, and biker's head smashes like a pumpkin. Better look for a car with a dent." "Look, Bumlinger," replied Shadow wearily, "this should be obvious even to you. This was no hit and run; this was a case of premeditated murder!" How was Barney murdered?

◆ Ioto Locomoto gently set his camera down as he bent over to shake the sand from his shoes and readjust his knee socks. Resuming his stroll along the beach, the professor continued to snap pictures of everything that moved and just about everything else that didn't. Several minutes later, Locomoto came upon a large crowd. Pushing through for a better view, Locomoto saw a very strange sight that just begged for a picture. It was his best picture of the day and probably the oddest. The picture he took showed three girls in swim-

suits. The strange part is that two of the girls were smiling but they were both very sad, and the third girl, who was crying, was very happy. What situation would make them behave in such a strange manner?

◆ "Listen, Shadow, Sally's life is on the line. They aren't bluffing," stammered Chip Dawson. "Is that Silicon Sally that's running your office?" inquired Shadow. "That was Sally," replied Chip. "Ain't she something?" "Well, I can certainly see how she came by her nickname," said Shadow as he read the ransom note: *"Dawson—You'll pay us $1million in seven days or your beloved Sally is a goner. We know everything about her. We'll be in touch."* "See," said an ashen-faced Chip Dawson, "Sally's life is hanging in thin air. I must have a couple of officers protecting her 24 hours a day. I count on her for everything. She basically runs my company." "I wish I could help you," replied Shadow, "but I'm afraid protecting Sally's life isn't in my jurisdiction. I have to run along because the Crabtree Pet Store was robbed last night and that's really a priority." Why would Sally's life rank below a simple pet-store robbery?

◆ "Gentlemen," began Art Bragg, "I've been in Brazil for the past two years and I've discovered the proverbial goose that lays the golden egg. These eggs are none other than banana plants. True to my genius, I've developed a strain of plant that grows wild, particularly where tropical forests have been felled. For pennies per acre I can purchase freshly cleared rain-forest land and plant my strain of cuttings. They grow faster than weeds and require no care. We simply pick 'em and ship 'em in specially designed containers. I purchased 20 acres of land, and I've harvested two crops since. This picture shows me and a couple of locals picking the second crop, which was snapped up by the U.S. markets. With $1 million invested now I can guarantee a return of 300% in one year!" It was then that Ari Gant declared, "Bragg, both you and your picture are obvious frauds." Why?

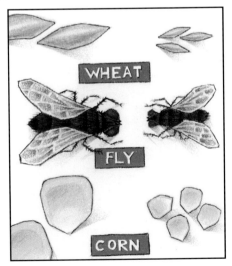

◆ Whenever Dee Septor, the world famous magician, went to a dinner party, and he sensed the hostess was just about to die of embarrassment because the party was as flat as her soufflé, it was a given that Dee, the party saver, would pull out the old knife-and-glass trick. "The task is this," challenged Dee. "Form an equilateral triangle with three identical glasses so that they are just slightly further apart than the length of three identical dinner knives. Now, using just the knives, and without moving the glasses, make a bridge between the three glasses that is strong enough to support a fourth glass full of water." How can this be done?

◆ "Gentlemen," began Professor Beaker, "my new discovery will revolutionize the world. I've found a completely natural way to enhance growth, whether it's for plants, insects, or humans. So far, I've only experimented on plants and insects, but the results speak for themselves. On the left you'll notice huge grains and kernels—not to mention the extraordinarily large house fly. On the right you can see a fly, wheat, and corn, which are anemic in comparison. Example, when the two flies emerged from the pupae, neither of them was bigger than the head of a small nail. Two weeks after ingesting my invention, the fly on the left has grown twice as fast as the fly on the right, which has eaten nothing but...well you know what flies like best." "I know what flies like best," interrupted Quantum, "and Beaker, you're full of it!" Why would Quantum say this?

◆ Miss Scarlet O'Hara was a wealthy widow who could easily be described as eccentric. She believed herself to be the incarnation of the famous character in the novel *Gone With the Wind*, and as a result, she tried to imitate her in every way. As strange as this fixation could be, in addition, everything she owned had to be white. Miss Scarlet instructed an architect to build her a huge white bungalow that had no less than twelve white bedrooms and twelve white bathrooms. Her stables were all to be painted white to match both the white house and the white garage. The principal feature of her home was naturally the grand staircase. With all things being equal, what color would Miss Scarlet have instructed her painters to paint the grand staircase?

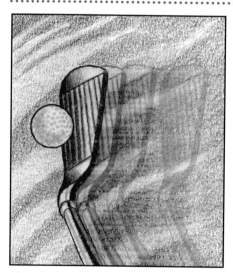

◆ Alan tried to ignore the television cameras and concentrate on the shot at hand. Holding the golf ball straight out, he dropped it into the dirt and pondered the most efficient way to strike the ball. Instead of using a sand wedge, he chose a specially designed six iron. With total concentration, he gripped the club firmly with one hand and gave a hard swing. The club dug deep into the dirt, sending the ball skittering several yards. Undaunted, he dropped a second ball, swung, and again the club head was off line, causing the ball to skitter only a short distance. Finally, with renewed determination, Alan dropped a third ball and drove it long and straight. "Out of this world," murmured his partner. Many golf reporters, analysts, and spectators described these three shots as the greatest shots the game of golf has ever known. Why?

◆ Charles Pompuss stopped off at the Soul-Ace Hotel for coffee. Always wanting to make an impression, Charles ordered coffee in his most debonair tone. "Monsieur, un cafe au lait, s'il vous plaît." "Listen, Mack," said the waiter, "we speak American here, so try again. What'll you have?" "A coffee with cream. Or a cuppuccino, my good man!" said Charles, rolling his eyes at the boorish waiter. "Listen, young man," continued Charles, "you should be grateful to people such as myself who could teach you a few things about culture. I speak five languages fluently. I learned Polish while spending two years there; then I moved to Holland for 6 months and learned Dutch. From there I learned Belgian while in that country, and just recently I returned from France where I became fluent in French." "Nice try, blowhard," replied the waiter, "but you're a bald-faced liar!" Why would he say that?

◆ Since it was Snorri's last night of bachelorhood, his friends Jon, Halldor, and Thorfin decided to take him downtown to Reykjavik, Iceland, to celebrate. Unfortunately for Snorri, he had a bit too much schnapps and eventually passed out. Seizing the moment, Halldor, an airplane pilot, decided to send him on a flight bound for Greece. Unlike Snorri's head, the night was perfectly clear. Not long after the plane had taken off, a bleary-eyed Snorri woke up to hear the pilot announce their destination—Greece! Still gathering his senses, Snorri gazed blankly out of the window to see a large city below. Instantly, he knew he was flying over London. How could he have known it was London?

◆ Art Bragg, Colonel Blackhead, and Dr. Prod were swapping war stories at the Soul-Ace Hotel. Art loved to recall how he won his medal when he and one of his carrier pigeons saved a platoon from certain ambush. "As you may or may not know," began Art, "carrier pigeons are able to fly in excess of 70 kilometers per hour for a number of hours. As it happens, I was at our temporary head-quarters when we intercepted an enemy transmission about an immi-nent ambush on our advancing troops. Immediately I attached the warning message to my prize carrier and sent him off to warn the platoon. Within hours, my carrier returned with a message that the troops would hold their position until reinforcements arrived." "What a cock-and-bull story that is," snorted Colonel Blackhead. Why?

◆ Ms. Tittle was in tears as she placed the little hamster cage on Dr. Probe's examining table. "I've taken Goldie to four veterinarians, and they've all told me that Goldie is simply dying of old age." Dr. Probe peered into the cage to see the little hamster looking the worse for wear. "Look, Dr. Probe, I'm a very wealthy lady. Please make her well; money is no object." At that, Dr. Probe stood up and said, "Well, Ms. Tittle, I've been experimenting with an aging rem-edy. The cure is expensive and risky, and I must admit that I haven't attempted it so far." "If that's Goldie's only chance . . . ," blubbered Tittle. Several days later, Tittle returned to find Goldie in good health. "Goldie took well to my treatment," agreed Dr. Probe, "but I fear that you're going to feel ill when you get my bill." How could Dr. Probe cure Goldie of the effects of old age?

◆ As Ioto Quantum carefully snapped his 34th picture that hour, he turned toward Professor Beaker and said, "You know, Beaker, I've seen both the enormous Cheops pyramid in Egypt and the Quetzalcoatl pyramid in Mexico, but this is even more impressive!" "Ladies and gentlemen," began the tour guide, "this is the largest construction project ever undertaken by man—modern or ancient. This American public works project began in 1947, and now covers over 3,000 acres. Upon its completion in 2005, it will rise to 435 feet at its peak. It's more than 25 times the size of the pyramid of Khufu in Egypt, and in total volume surpasses the Great Wall of China. It employs more than 500 people, many of whom are responsible for planting and caring for the more than 50,000 trees and shrubs it boasts." What great construction project were the professors touring?

◆ This was Gloria Goody's second date with Charles Pompuss, and she swore it would be her last. "For our third date, Gloria," began Charles, "I think we'll go camping with my family. I'm a natural outdoorsman, you know." "Charles, I would love to, but the last time I went camping I had a horrible experience. First, I was eaten alive by mosquitoes and a bear attacked my tent while I was attempting to sleep. Panicking, I ran through the woods only to cross the path of a porcupine and her young. As I tried to back away, she fired 5 or 6 quills into my stomach. The pain was excruciating. By now, I was ready to go back to the tent to face the bear. I found my keys and drove to the nearest hospital, vowing to never go camping again." "If you don't want to go camping, just say so. You don't have to make up a phony story," replied Charles. What didn't he believe?

◆ The early settlers on the Isle of Begile were a rather conservative group who established the island's bylaws. One of the first laws passed was that all the men were to be clean-shaven, and furthermore, no man was allowed to shave himself. To make matters even more trying, the bylaws stipulated that all men had to be shaved by a licensed barber. For whatever reason, the Isle only issued one barber's license, and that was to an elder who was nearing eighty years of age. Strangely enough, everything seemed to work, until an immigrant lawyer arrived on the scene and asked the overlooked question, "If no man is allowed to shave himself, who then shaves the barber?" How did the Begilers avoid this paradox?

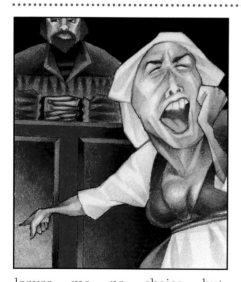

◆ "I couldn't watch her 24 hours a day," sobbed the mother of the murder victim. "I allowed little Chantelle to play in the village street as long as there were other children around. I never dreamt that she would actually be murdered by *them!*" she screamed, pointing at the accused and her family, who stood in the prisoner's dock. When the judge asked to hear the prisoner's defense, she refused to talk. The judge implored her to defend herself so that he might lighten her sentence, but the accused merely grunted. "Your silence leaves me no choice but to condemn you to death by hanging. Although your offspring participated in this heinous crime, I'm going to spare them punishment. Not having a mother in today's world is punishment enough." Although the accused was perfectly healthy, she never uttered a word in defense. Why not?

◆ "I've eaten in the finest restaurants in the world," said Art Bragg to his girl-friend, "and this place is the best." Just then the maître d' approached Bragg and, with a disdain he reserved for all his customers, asked if they had reservations. Art went to slip him $5 and the maître d' stepped back, fearing he might get some of Art Bragg on himself. After being seated, Art announced that he would order for the little lady, since he knew what was best. Just after lunch, both Art and his girlfriend began looking a little green around the gills. When asked about dessert, Art mumbled a reply and suddenly threw up all over the table. Fortunately, his girlfriend made it to the washroom in time. In fact, almost everyone who ate lunch at the restaurant was sick. Since there wasn't anything wrong with the food, what could possibly have happened?

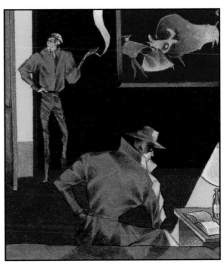

◆ "Let's go back to your room and hear your story again," said Shadow as he removed the Do Not Disturb sign and groped about for the light switch. The bedside light came on, casting a warm glow on an opened Bible. Shadow sat on one of the beds, and Shady leaned against the wall. "Okay," sighed Shadow, "Give me the whole story again." "For the fifth time," replied Shady, "I was lying in bed reading the Bible when I heard a loud commotion followed by two gunshots. I opened my door and peered down the hall, only to see the back of a woman going down the fire escape. She had a gun in her hand, and she wore a red kerchief. I tore across the hall to Sam's room only to find him lying facedown on the floor. When I turned him over to see if he was alive, hotel security burst in and accused me of murder." "Based on that story so do I," said Shadow. Why?

◆ The search for the infamous Northwest Passage seemed as elusive as the mythical Holy Grail. It wasn't until 1906, when Roald Amundsen followed the Canadian coast to Cape Nome, Alaska, that an official passage was finally declared. Ironically, however, the first ship to actually traverse the Northwest Passage was the Octavius nearly 150 years earlier. In 1762, the Octavius was frozen in, north of Alaska, and was forced to wait out the winter. Thirteen years later, in 1775, she and her crew were hailed off the coast of Greenland. Since the Octavius was more than 100 years ahead of Amundsen, why weren't Amundsen and his crew credited with this famous discovery?

◆ "Sid Shady's going to try to smuggle the stolen paintings out of the country tonight. How he's going to do it is any-body's guess, but suspect anything," stated Shadow to the assembled security. "We all know what the *Mona Lisa* looks like, and that is, of course, the one painting we *must* have safely returned." That night Shadow was contacted by airport officials, saying that they had caught a disguised Shady attempting to board a plane. "He used his regular passport," said the guard, "and he almost slipped through. He was wear-ing a wig, a phony mustache, and he even sported a deep dark tan. He also had the *Mona Lisa*. It was rolled up with a bunch of architectural drawings. Get this, he still claims he's innocent and that we can't hold him. Do you believe this guy?" "He's right," said Shadow, "we can't hold him." Why not?

◆ Just after the conclusion of the Second World War, Harpo, who was both deaf and mute, was looking to take a train from Chicago to Detroit. His plan was to do a little shopping in Motown and return to Chicago later the same day. Harpo looked up above the ticket counter and read the sign that said:

Chicago to Detroit	50¢
Round Trip	$1.00

Without communicating in any way, Harpo put a dollar on the ticket counter, and the clerk automatically gave him a round-trip ticket. How could the clerk have known that Harpo wanted a two-way ticket?

◆ Dee Septor, the world-famous magician, was visiting the town of Magicoque for the annual cheese festival, when he remembered his famous cheese trick. When the three finalists were chosen for Best Cheese in Show, Dee approached the judges' table and announced that he would grace the crowd with his cheese trick. Dee took the three prized cheeses and then requested three hats from the crowd. He then placed a hat over each of the three cheeses. Without another word Dee lifted the first hat and ate the

cheese. After a sip of water he then ate the second. As the crowd grew tense, Dee raised his hand, asking for calm and patience. Dee then lifted the third hat and ate that cheese as well. "Mesdames et messieurs, before your very eyes, and without getting sick, I will now put all three pieces of cheese that I have just eaten under one of these three hats." How?

◆ Sid Shady lay dead on the bed. The murder weapon, the pillow, had been removed from his face to check for breath. A violent struggle had taken place as evidenced by the torn pillow and the feathers scattered about the room. Shadow reviewed the recent events. Shady, who had been implicated in the murder of a local union boss, had suddenly agreed to cooperate with the police. While being transferred, an assassin's bullet tore through his shoulder. Shady was rushed to the hospital, the bullet was removed, and he was recovering under the guard of Constable Bumlinger. The constable later testified that nothing had been brought in or out of the room and that Shady's only visitor had been his doctor. "When the doctor left, I opened the door to check on him," said Bumlinger, "and that's when I saw the gruesome scene." "Bumlinger's obviously lying," said Shadow. How does he know?

◆ Art Bragg smiled contentedly as he glanced at his rear-view mirror and watched the lake grow smaller. It was the fall of 1965, and Art was sure it had to be this year's record. He loved to feel the little pulls and jerks on the wheel of his truck each time the boat's trailer hit a small bump. The tall pines seemed to go on forever as Art anxiously scanned the countryside for a telephone. When he finally spotted one, Art quickly pulled over and made the call he so desperately wanted to make. It was the last twenty-five cents Art Bragg ever spent. He was found a short time later lying among the broken glass—dead. The telephone handset hung from its cord. Since foul play wasn't a factor, how did Art die?

♦ Constable Bumlinger enjoyed strutting through the Begile open-air market and helping himself to whatever fresh fruit and vegetables struck his fancy. It was just about the time that Bumlinger tried to swallow his third free peach that an expertly launched tomato struck the back of his head, dislodging the fruit from his mouth. Furious, Bumlinger whirled around to see Sam, Barney, Sid, and Art—each looking like the cat that had swallowed the canary. Bumlinger immediately stomped over to the quartet. "Whoever threw that tomato deserves to be kicked in the head by a donkey, and I'm just the one to do it!" screamed Bumlinger. Sam said that Sid threw it. Barney claimed he was innocent. Sid accused Art of throwing it. Art exclaimed that that was a lie. Since only one of them told the truth, who threw the tomato?

♦ Professor Quantum, the quintessential absent-minded professor, was so engrossed in reading the back of a book while he walked toward the counter, he almost walked into a wall and three innocent people on the way. Once there, Quantum finished his reading and handed the book to the attendant. Taking the book, she said, "I know you, you're my history prof!" Quantum squinted his eyes and, searching his memory in vain, replied, "Of course I recognize you; I didn't realize you worked here." They both knew he didn't recall seeing her, but the young woman didn't really expect him to. She flipped the book over and told him that it would cost $27.50. Quantum handed her $40, received his change, and walked out without the book. Why would the attendant let him leave without his book?

◆ "There's been a report that your car was involved in a hit and run this morning," said Shadow as Barney Dribble answered his door. "I haven't driven my car in two days," replied Barney. Just then Bertha Dribble appeared and demanded to know what was going on. Shadow smiled at the comical-looking couple. Bertha towered nearly 2 feet above her 5-foot husband. "Now look here, Shadow! Barney came home from work two days ago and that car hasn't moved since." "Just the same, I'd like to see it," said Shadow. Bertha grabbed the

keys and stormed out to the garage. "There, look to your heart's content," she snarled. "In the light," said Shadow. Furious, Bertha jumped behind the wheel, revved the engine, and squealed the tires in reverse. "Satisfied?!" screamed Bertha, stomping towards the house. "You two are obviously lying to me," said Shadow. Why would he say that?

◆ "I don't care if you are Sir Arthur Braggs," continued Shadow. "After distinctly hearing a shot, I rowed my boat across to see you riding out of the woods with a dead duck in your carrier. Since the bird has just been shot, I can't help but be suspicious." "Now look here," replied Arthur, "I moored my motor yacht in this cove last night. This morning, I went for a bicycle ride and stopped for coffee at the Soul-Ace Hotel. I'm sure the proprietor remembers me because, while there, someone stole my pump and saddlebags. Luckily I had my backpack containing my tire repair kit. Anyway, about 20 minutes ago, my tire blew, which is what you thought was a gunshot. I repaired my tire and was on my way when I saw this dead duck. I was taking it back to my motor yacht so it wouldn't go to waste." "That story is a lie!" Shadow said. Why?

◆ Professor Herring pulled up a chair and said, "If you're looking to fill the head faculty position of English History, then I'm the one to straighten this department out." "Fate must be smiling on me, Professor," said Quantum, "since there's a charity auction tonight, and I could use the advice of an expert." Herring looked at the auction list and commented that half the items were rubbish and the other half were likely overpriced. "Well, it is for charity," suggested Quantum, "and I must buy something." Herring looked at the list again and said, "The best buy is the handwritten letter in Old English by King George I. That would be valuable. The only other two items of value would be a wig worn by Queen Elizabeth I, and a second document, a letter written by the Duke of Bedford and addressed to Queen Elizabeth I, Buckingham Palace." "Herring," stated Quantum, "you're a fraud." Why would he say that?

◆ Dan Manley carefully guided the big ship into the dock. Satisfying himself that she was secure, he struggled out of his work clothes and tried to relax after the long day. Dan couldn't put his finger on it, but there was some lingering anxiety about the job done earlier that day. While sipping a coffee, he reread the job outline and the detailed analysis of what needed to be completed. Dan looked out the window while thinking about the day's events, when to his horror, he noticed his co-worker accidentally tear his suit. Dan knew his

friend would be dead in a matter of moments. Since Dan's co-worker was not shot and he didn't stab himself, what could have happened to him that would have been so catastrophic?

◆ "Fill 'er up," hollered the taxi driver to the gas attendant. "I'm sorry, mister," said the driver to his passenger, "I know you're a pilot and you've got a flight to make, but if I don't get some gas we'll never get there." Realizing the urgency of the situation, the taxi driver handed the attendant a $50 bill and sped off, not bothering to wait for change. Several minutes later they came to a screeching halt in the airport terminal. The pilot dropped a twenty onto the front seat and dashed off toward the plane. As the pilot checked his craft, he realized his aircraft fuel tank was also low on fuel. Not wanting to fall behind schedule, the pilot put some bananas, apples, bread rolls, and water into his fuel tank and took off. Several hours later he landed as planned. How could the engine have functioned with such a bizarre mixture in the tank?

◆ Shadow watched in glum silence as the two ambulance attendants lifted the lifeless body of Mrs. Sham onto the stretcher. "This was the very reason I didn't want to teach her to climb," sobbed Sam Sham. "I realize it's a bad time," consoled Shadow, "but for the record, I must know exactly what happened." "On my instructions," began Sam, "my wife drove a piton into the top of the rock face and secured the line to it. Then she secured the other end to her waist and began to let herself down using the line. Suddenly, she lost her composure and panicked. She started to swing back and forth. The line must have been rubbing against the rock because suddenly it snapped and she fell to her death. I immediately ran to my car and called 911." "Based on that story," said Shadow, "I'm going to charge you with murder." Why?

◆ "That last meal is sitting in my stomach like a rock," murmured James. Turning his attention to the man before him, James exclaimed, "You've got to be kidding, my good man. You expect me to tip you for your services?!" "Well, it is customary, and besides, without tips I could barely feed my wife and children." "That's scarcely my concern," retorted James. "At any rate you've got your nerve asking for a tip before you've done your job." "True," replied John, "but I know from experience that my only means of getting a tip is collecting before I do my job. Besides, it provides incentive." James soon saw the logic in John's argument and gave him a handful of gold coins. "I've no axe to grind with you. Besides, I've got more money than I can spend anyway. Farewell, and I thank you in advance for a job done swiftly," said James. What service was James tipping for?

◆ "I, Jacques, made her and this circus! Look at this," hissed Jacques, shoving the show bill under Shadow's face. "Do you see any mention of Jacques? No! Only Josephine! Men love her, the women and children think she's adorable. She was nobody when I found her. Pierre, the circus owner, refused to pay me for teaching her. He said she was untrainable and wouldn't amount to anything. But I bring her in and teach her how to eat, how to act, and how to walk a high wire like a cat! Then Pierre sees her perform, sees the crowds go crazy, and suddenly Jacques is out." "Tell me," demanded Shadow, "did you rig the tightrope on which Josephine last walked?" "It was I," said Jacques, sobbing. "But you can't arrest me for murder; I only wanted her to fall and hurt herself. I didn't mean for her to die." "You disgust me," said Shadow. "Luckily for you I can't arrest you for murder." Why not?

◆ Sid Shady placed another envelope in the pile and went back outside to wait in the alley. "It's a veritable delivery service," chuckled Shady to himself. Shady just loved Fridays because Fridays were payday, and today was Friday. Shady stood in the shadows and watched several people make withdrawals from the cash machine. Inside the building, a bored security guard watched the customers go through their transactions and leave without incident. As Shady's next victim opened the door and stepped outside, he stumbled

into Shady's waiting arms. Propping the man's arm around his shoulder, Sid helped him around the corner and down the alley, where he dumped him next to his other victims. Shady gingerly removed the man's cash, and, like a spider in its web, he waited for the next unsuspecting customer. How was Shady robbing his victims?

◆ High over the jungle, General Tick focused his binoculars as he studied the tiny antlike figures below. Tick noted the scouting parties moving out from their base as they desperately sought to determine the size and location of the enemy. "Let's go before we're spotted," snapped Tick. The next morning, Tick observed the raging battle below. "I've been in combat for years, and I've never seen such desperate fighting!" The general had just witnessed the use of chemical sprays resulting in thousands of casualties. There were so many dead that neither side bothered digging graves. They simply carried the dead to a refuse pile. Later, the victorious army rounded up hundreds of slaves and engaged them in every reprehensible activity imaginable, including child slave labor. Although this was a battle of major proportions, the press never bothered to report it. Why not?

◆ It happened in Somerset, England, in 1685. "Master, master, wonderful news!" screamed the servant boy. "The king himself has commissioned you to paint the portrait of James, Duke of Monmouth!" "This is wonderful news," said the old painter Kneller. "It'll bring a fine commission. Quick, get my paints and supplies, we must go at once." When they arrived at the castle and were brought before the duke, neither Kneller nor the duke bothered to exchange a single word, much less pleasantries. Kneller studied the duke's profile for a moment and then mumbled to himself as he rummaged through his paints and supplies. Suddenly Kneller exclaimed, "Boy, you forgot to pack the needle and thread. I can't possibly paint the duke's portrait without them!" Why would he need a needle and thread to paint the portrait?

◆ It was in 1794 that William Congreve and his eccentric girlfriend, Henrietta, Duchess of Marlborough, were throwing their annual New Year's Eve bash. The arriving guests were met by Henrietta before being ushered into the banquet hall to greet William Congreve, the great English playwright. Even though Congreve never bothered to utter a single word to his guests, nobody seemed to take any offense; they simply got quietly giddy. Things changed radically, however, when Congreve's doctor, who was in good

form, declared that he couldn't recall ever having seen Congreve look healthier or more relaxed than he did that evening. Henrietta smiled approvingly at both the doctor and Congreve while the guests tried their best not to go into complete hysterics. Why would the doctor's comments be considered so funny?

◆ The only "sport" Beulah Buttinski ever mastered was bingo. In fact, Beulah studiously avoided exercise at all costs. Considering the above facts, Beulah had a very strange habit. On Monday, Wednesday, and Friday Beulah took the bus to the local bingo hall. The bus always made two stops close to the hall. The first stop was 330 feet (100 meters) away and the second stop was 660 feet (200 meters) away. Strangely enough, Beulah always got out at the second stop and walked the 200 meters. What reason could she have had for walking the extra distance?

◆ "Hit this bank up here," said Sam Sham to Sid Shady. Shady brought the car to a screeching halt as Sam jumped out and ran inside. Needing some quick cash rather than the mother lode, Sam decided he would settle for whatever he could get. Sam had no idea how many people he held up, and moments later, with a handful of cash, he dashed out of the bank, almost pushing the door off its hinges. Suddenly, Sam felt a wave of nausea sweep over him as he saw his old nemesis Detective Shadow viewing the entire scene. Instantly, Sam's worst fear was realized when he saw that Shadow's car was parked right in front of their getaway car. Resigning himself to the worst, Sam threw up his hands. Just then Shadow's emergency pager went off, and seconds later he ran to his car and sped off. Why would Shadow leave without an arrest?

◆ Barney Dribble nervously looked out the plane's window to see the mountains looming in the distance. He closed his eyes and concentrated on the steady drone of the plane's propellers, which seemed to have a soothing effect. Just then, he heard the unmistakable voice of his wife, Bertha. "Thought you'd get away from Bertha, did ya?!" The other passengers gasped as an obviously crazed Bertha Dribble began waving a handgun around. "Unless I get that briefcase now, nobody gets off this plane alive, least of all a worm like you, Barney." Barney suddenly thought he'd lost command of his body. He felt himself get out of his seat and lunge for the door. In one swift motion Barney unlocked the latch, pushed the door open, and jumped. When Barney eventually hit the ground, he was miraculously alive. Since he didn't have a parachute, how could he have survived?

◆ Today was a big day in the anguished life of Barney Dribble. For years he had been selling Suction Unlimited vacuum cleaners door to door, but today, it would all change. Barney was invited to give his pitch in front of the Women for Freedom movement. In Barney's mind, sales would be as easy as shooting fish in a barrel. Barney stopped by the office to grab several thousand order forms, when he realized he was running late. "Help me load these vacuums!" begged Barney to Art Bragg, the office manager. As Barney sped off, Art

hollered, "Drive carefully, Barney, or you'll lose your license!" Barney's perspiring hands clutched the wheel as he mentally rehearsed his speech for the hundredth time. Suddenly, Barney pulled his car to the side of the road, got out, and ran away. Why would Barney abandon his car, his vacuums, and the opportunity to make his speech?

◆ "I have mixed emotions about July 4th," said Sid Shady. "I'm patriotic and all, but that's the day I lost my fifth wife. We always celebrated July 4th in a different part of the country. Being avid climbers, we went to northern Alaska to climb Mount Doonerak. As dusk set in after the first day's climb, we made camp. It was a clear night with a billion stars in the sky. Being the patriotic romancer, I decided to surprise my wife and set off a fireworks display. I went out of sight to launch the first one. After her initial shock she was screaming with delight. After several more I heard a distant roar in the background. Much to my horror, I had started an avalanche. I managed to escape since I was on a cliff protected by a huge overhang." Sam Sham suddenly grabbed Shady's arm and whispered, "I suggest you never tell that tale again or you'll be arrested for murder!" What was wrong with Sid's story?

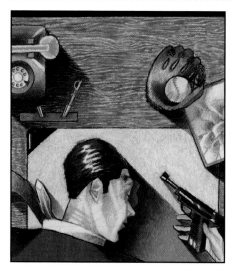

◆ Shadow arrived at the gruesome scene only to hear Constable Bumlinger telling the press that it was a clear case of suicide. Dan Manley, the famous baseball pitcher, was slumped over his desk— dead. A small puddle of blood had pooled near his head. Powder burns were evident on the right temple, indicating he was shot at close range. Dan's right hand, which rested on the desk, loosely held the gun that killed him. Shadow noted a suicide note which read:

"I know I was responsible for losing the World Series. I can no longer live with myself. I apologize to my teammates, my fans, and my family. Farewell."

Shadow recalled that Dan's two passions were gambling and pitching, with the latter clearly being his strength. Due to Dan's publicized gambling losses, and the evidence at the scene, Shadow concluded that this was a case of murder. What led him to that conclusion?

◆ In the 16th century, travelers to Turkey discovered the tulip. Struck by the flower's beauty, they brought it back to Holland, and it was soon sold throughout Europe. By the early 17th century, tulips were immensely fashionable, which caused a speculative frenzy that defied logic. Cultivated tulips occasionally produced striking mutations, caused by a virus, which soon led to perfect bulbs' becoming breeders. One Viceroy bulb sold for 4 oxen, 8 pigs, 12 sheep, 2 hogsheads of wine, 6 loads of rye, 4 barrels of beer, 2 barrels of butter, a half ton of cheese, and 2 carriages with 8 horses. When a shoemaker managed to grow a black flower, he was visited by growers from Haarlem who purchased it for 1,500 florins. Immediately after the sale, the new owners dropped the flower on the floor and ground it to a pulp. What would account for such strange behavior?

◆ Professor Quantum led Belvedere to the exhibit of Botticelli, the famous 15th century painter. "Describe *Madonna of the Rose Bush,*" requested Belvedere. "It's approximately 50 × 25 inches, and it shows the Madonna holding her baby. The colors are brilliant, and naturally prominent is the familiar pomegranate, his favorite motif." "Yes," said Belvedere, "it's one of the symbols of the Passion." The next painting Quantum described was Tintoretto's *The Last Supper.* "Again the colors are vibrant, and of course it shows Jesus

with his disciples. The rough table features several bowls of oranges, grapes, and dates." Quantum went on describing the painting and answering any questions Belvedere had. As they walked away from *The Last Supper,* Belvedere commented that Tintoretto may have been a brilliant painter, but he knew little of history. Why would he say that?

◆ The year was 1483 and Sir Henry Wyatt, a noble at the court of King Richard III, had been accused of being active in the recent uprising against the king. "You aren't even worthy of being hanged, you ungrateful dog!" screamed the enraged king. "I sentence you to die of starvation in the Tower of London. You can spend the last couple of weeks of your wretched life thinking of what you've done. If anyone should so much as dare to bring you a morsel of food, I will have his hands chopped off." Sir Henry was confined to a low, narrow cell, where he sat and awaited his inevitable fate. Miraculously, however, Sir Henry must have had nine lives, for after several months he was still in reasonably good health. Since no man had visited or brought him any food, how could he have managed to stay alive?

◆ It was in Rome, Italy, that Sid Shady slipped the plastic bag over Sam Sham's head. Sam struggled violently but soon succumbed. Shady then dragged Sam's body out to the garage and shoved him in the car's front seat. He opened the car's windows, then wrote a short suicide note and placed it on the dash. Shady started the car, closed the garage door, and wandered off to town. Hours later, Sam's body was discovered by the butler, who immediately called the Italian police. Constable Giuseppe examined the scene and declared that the poor fellow must have killed himself by carbon-monoxide poisoning. "Ah, too bad," said Giuseppe, "The suicide note, she is in a English. I no can read." "You stupido!" said the inspector, who took one look at the car and declared, "This is an obvious case of murder." How did the inspector know Sam Sham didn't commit suicide?

◆ Shadow reluctantly finished his doughnut and walked outside into the sweltering heat. Getting into his cruiser, he heard an urgent call that a black Corvette, heading towards the beach, had just dangerously sped through town. "Sounds like Sam Sham's car," thought Shadow, as he turned on his siren and raced to the beach, where he spotted Sam's car. Shadow walked to the water and found Sam and his girlfriend sunning themselves. When Shadow asked Sam for his license and his recent whereabouts, Sam replied that his license was in the car and that he'd been on the beach all day. Sam muttered under his breath as he walked to his car and unlocked it. Sitting in the driver's seat, Sam leaned over and snatched the license from the glove box. Shadow took a quick look at the license and said, "Sam you're lying about your whereabouts." How could he be so sure?

◆ Every fall the Soul-Ace Hotel saw the pilgrimage of the Blue Hair Society in their quest to watch the leaves change color. They counted their nickels and drank dangerously large quantities of tea, but otherwise were no trouble — except this year. One of their number was a thief. Hotel rooms were invaded; wallets, purses, and dentures were stolen. The Soul-Ace called Shadow. He ordered dinner in his room, where he could devise his plan of capture in solitude. It seemed to be a mistake. First the maid came in to deliver fresh tow-

els. Then a newlywed couple, locked in embrace, accidentally entered his room before making an apologetic departure. Next, an elderly lady knocked and entered, then apologized when she saw it was Shadow's room and not hers. Then room service knocked, bringing Shadow his dinner. Halfway through dinner, Shadow suddenly knew who his prime suspect was. Who?

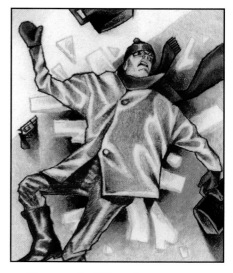

◆ "Okay, Slug," said Shadow, "Give me the story again—from the top." "Look," said Slug, "Barney Dribble used to work at my club up there on the tenth floor. I fired him a couple of weeks ago. Caught him scamming the till. He swore he didn't steal nothin'. Tonight he comes in, telling me that since he was fired for stealing, he might as well do it. Next thing I know he pulls out a gun and demands I open the safe and fill his two cases with cash. I do exactly as he says. After the cases are full, he starts to back out toward the door. Just then, my chief bouncer, Moe, walks into the room and sees Barney holding the gun at me. Moe goes berserk. As Barney turns toward the door, Moe just picks him up and throws him through the window with the cash, the gun, and all." "That story's going to need a lot of work," replied Shadow. Why?

◆ Dan Manley had just been given notice that his job at the One Mile Nuclear Power Plant was terminated. Dan took the news hard. He had been a loyal employee for 30 years, and now, just like that, he was out of a job. Although Dan was known for having a violent temper, he'd always been a model citizen who was among the first to volunteer for any number of community events. Two nights after his termination, Dan Manley, wielding an axe, broke into the head offices of the One Mile Nuclear Power Plant. Since there was nobody in the office, Dan hooked up a hose and sprayed the company computers, office records, and files, causing hundreds of thousands of dollars' damage. Within hours, the One Mile Plant found out about Dan's destruction and ironically agreed to hire him back. Why?

◆ Nurse Deadpan scolded Dr. Prod, the chief surgeon at Begile General, as she helped him into his gown. "Where have you been? We looked everywhere for you Doctor." "I was calling my bookie," joked Prod. Deep down he was concerned about his own health. For several days he'd been experiencing dizzy spells, which he hoped were due to stress and fatigue. "You know we can't perform this operation without you," continued Deadpan as she and Dr. Prod hurried into surgery. As soon as Prod entered the operating room, however, he blacked out. Immediately the available nurses and doctors rushed to attend him. When Prod regained consciousness and asked about the surgery, nurse Deadpan informed him that it had been a complete success. Since they had to have Dr. Prod, how could they have operated without him?

◆ Sam Slug was not a well-liked man. It would be safe to say that the majority of people who knew Sam passionately hated him. It was equally safe to say that Sam couldn't have cared less. "Happy July 4th," murmured Sam as he jabbed the hook through the worm's eye and tossed it over the side of the boat. Not far away, Sid Shady was loading his rifle. Sid knew Sam Slug, and as far as Sid was concerned, he could be safely counted among the majority. Several minutes later Sam Slug was dead. The cause of death was a bullet

wound through the top of his head. Sam never saw Sid; in fact, he never even heard the shot. Although Detective Shadow eventually determined that the bullet came from Sid Shady's rifle, Sid was never charged. Why not?

◆ Sid Shady decided to kill Sam Sham, and he would do it today, on Sam's birthday. Relieving Sam of his rotten life wasn't a half-bad birthday present, thought Sid. He would pose as a singing birthday-gram and finish Sam off in his own backyard. The neighbor recounted to Shadow, "I was gardening when I looked up to see a guy in a strange out-fit entering Sam's backyard, and moments later I heard popping sounds, like champagne corks, which reminded me that it was Sam's birthday. As I was going over to wish Sam well, the singer-guy started screaming that Sam had been shot. I picked up Sam's cellular phone and called 911. The singer-guy said that just as he'd entered the back-yard, he'd seen a man climbing over the wall. It must have been the killer, because nobody, including your officers, can locate the murder weapon!" How did Shady dispose of the gun?

◆ Sam Sham answered his door to see Shadow standing in the blowing snow. "Come in," said Sam, "but don't expect it to be much warmer in here yet with my power having been cut. Like I said on the phone, I've been robbed. I was away on business for the past week, and I just got home a few hours ago to find my house freezing. Look at my aquarium! The fish aren't swimming, 'cause it's a solid block of ice! I had the power line repaired but I didn't realize it had been deliberately cut until later. Want a coffee?" asked Sam, filling the kettle. "As I was saying, after my power line was fixed, I took an ice-cold shower and went to bed. I woke an hour later and suddenly noticed that my picture safe was slightly ajar and all my jewelry was gone. That's when I realized the burglars must have cut the power to disengage my alarm. "Nice try, Sam," replied Shadow, "but you're obviously lying." About what?

◆ It is well known that the early Egyptians were both superstitious and devoutly religious. They held many things and beings as sacred, and foremost among these were domesticated cats. When a cat died in a home, all the members of the household shaved their eyebrows in mourning. In ancient Egypt, cats were even buried in special mausoleums with mummified mice for their afterlife. When King Cambyses II of Persia invaded Egypt in 525 B.C., he was well aware of the Egyptians' sacred beliefs. When his army was confronted with the impenetrable walls of Memphis, Cambyses suddenly had a brilliant idea. He had his army round up as many domesticated cats as it could and used them to force the Egyptians to surrender their city. How were the cats used to open the city's gates?

◆ Mark O'Connor had been born and raised on a New Zealand sheep ranch, which left him unaccustomed to large crowds or the random violence of city life.

Minutes ago, Mark had been enjoying the beautiful day, and now he suddenly found himself running for his life. His legs felt like rubber. Unable to push through the crowd made him feel as though he were suspended in that dreamlike state of slow motion. Instinctively, he knew he was about to die. His killer had singled him out in a

blind rage. Mark tried to run in a zigzag pattern, but it proved futile. Mark's back was the bull's-eye. He heard a loud scream, then felt the white hot pain of being stabbed. He died almost instantly. Although a local policeman witnessed Mark's murder, he did nothing to apprehend the killer. Why not?

◆ Don Sandino scanned the bookie's reports and looked up at Sam Sluguchi sitting across the desk. "It looks as if Tony is skimming off the top," sighed Don Sandino wearily. "I don't know what he thinks! What—I won't find out?! I hate to give an order like this since he's my only nephew, but business is business. No exceptions!" "It will be done, Don Sandino," whispered Sam. Two days later, Sam Sluguchi held a gun to Tony's head and asked him if he had any last words. "Who gave you the order to do this," questioned Tony, "my only

uncle?" "It wasn't your uncle," replied Sam. "He's been in a coma for 3 weeks and he likely won't come out. Have a nice trip," quipped Sam as he pulled the trigger. Since Sam told the truth about Tony's uncle being in a coma, who could have given the order to kill Tony?

◆ Sam Sham and his wife Sandy waited in their driveway for an opening in the heavy traffic. "It's like this every morning," grumbled Sam. "I sit here for 5 minutes just waiting to get into the waiting traffic." "Don't get so uptight," warned Sandy. "You've got to watch your ulcer." Spotting an opening, Sam backed the little sports car onto the road, quickly threw it into first gear, and sped away with the car's tires squealing. "Take it easy," warned Sandy. "So what are you making for dinner tonight?" inquired Sam. "Reservations," mumbled Sandy, looking out her window. A short time later, Sam drove through an intersection and crashed head-on into a garbage truck that had just run a red. Sam flew through the windshield. Sandy, who was unhurt, was almost hysterical while she tried to dial 911. When she was asked exactly where the accident occurred, Sandy couldn't say. Why not?

◆ The house was dark when Sid Shady pressed the doorbell. When there was no answer, he went around the back of the house and removed the screen from the window. Taking a screwdriver from his pocket, he managed to jimmy the latch free and slowly slide the window open. Shady tucked his gun in the back of his pants and with one quick leap he grabbed the windowsill and pulled himself into the house. Shady crawled forward on his hands until his legs followed him in. Just then, he saw the outline of a figure moving in the dark. His right hand instinctively reached back for his gun just as the shadowy figure's left hand also reached for a gun. Shady fired a single shot at the figure, who quickly disappeared. Strangely enough, neither the shooting nor the break-and-enter was ever reported. Why not?

◆ Detective Shadow felt around in the vagrant's pockets for some I.D. but found nothing. "Like I told you," drawled Bumlinger, explaining the obvious, "this bum was trying to snitch a free ride out West like all the other derelicts heading to California for the winter. He failed to hang on, so he got what was coming—a smashed-in head. Case closed." Shadow tried his best to block out the noise emanating from Bumlinger's mouth as he examined the dead man's hands. Surprisingly they had been recently manicured.

Squinting into the setting sun, he saw what looked like a briefcase about 150 feet (50 meters) away. Shadow picked up the case and snapped it open to find several thousand dollars along with the man's I.D. and a pair of prescription glasses. "Even for you, Bumlinger," sighed Shadow, "this should have been an obvious case of foul play." Why?

◆ Detective Shadow got out of his car and was walking toward the dead deer lying in the middle of the road when he noticed a car in the ditch. Shadow ran down to the car and opened the door. He immediately recognized that it was Sam Slug. Sam had a huge gash on his forehead, and his clothes were covered in blood. Shadow noticed the steering wheel was badly bent to one side where Sam's head must have hit. Shadow checked Sam's neck for a pulse and quickly determined that Sam Slug and the deer had met the same fate. Shadow struggled back up the muddy embankment to his car and called in to headquarters. "This is Detective Shadow. I've got a dead deer and a murder victim in a 1997 dark blue Cadillac. I'm at . . ." Why would Shadow think that Sam Slug had been murdered?

◆ Pegleg stumbled up the shore and fell on the beach, exhausted but happy. He was the sunken ship's navigator and sole survivor. Taking stock of his situation, Pegleg established that he was all alone on a lush tropical island. Although things could be worse, it was a tad too isolated for a permanent settlement. A search of the island turned up a ball of fishing line, 6 fish hooks, and 3 empty bottles labeled root beer, cola, and ginger ale. With these materials, Pegleg decided to send a message for help. Realizing that a corkless bottle would get swamped in the waves, Pegleg ingeniously inscribed a help message on one of the labels, and using the other materials he sent it safely out to sea. How did he do it?

◆ The warm tropical sun beat down on Yukio Takushi as he wiped the sweat from his brow and tightened the last lug nut on the wheel. Leaning against a palm tree, he looked admiringly at the shiny vehicle with the new plow and snow tires. "Sometimes I think you should have married your truck," joked Yukio's wife, Amy. Just then the truck's phone rang. It was Yukio's boss warning him of an approaching storm. "The new plow and tires came at just the right time," noted Yukio. "You and I have never been out of the United States, Amy. If it storms enough this season, perhaps we can save enough to go to Europe in the fall. And on that note, I had better go and battle this oncoming storm," said Yukio as he grabbed his coat and boots and jumped in his truck. "I should be back in about three or four hours," he shouted, driving off in a cloud of "tropical" dust. What was Yukio's job?

◆ Barney Dribble was glued to the TV as he watched the ponies thunder up the field. "I see you enjoy polo," said Art Bragg, pulling up a chair. "For your kind, Barney, polo will never be more than a spectator sport. Playing is for nobility and other well-bred people. Did you know that I'm one of the top players in the country? The key to polo is being able to control the pony with the left hand while focusing on the ball's direction. You've got 8 human brains and 8 horse brains doing 16 different things. That's where breeding

and horsemanship are key. Hey, I just happen to have some pictures. Here's one of the national team. I'm not shown since I was teaching King Fahad that day. Here's another picture with me about to score the winning goal." Just then Shadow looked over Bragg's shoulder and said, "Bragg, that photo is a fake and so are you." Why?

◆ Shadow surveyed the barren showroom of Shady Picture photography store. "Let me get this straight," began Shadow. "One week ago you buy this store and immediately triple the insurance coverage of the previous owner. Then last night you're mysteriously robbed of all your stock, is that it?" "Precisely," replied Shady, "and I can prove it. My cousin Twyla is visiting me from Ohio. Last night after leaving the drive-in, I suggested I take her picture in front of my new store. Since it was dark, I had to use my flash. Luckily, I did. As I was developing the pictures at home last night, I noticed in the background the outline of a man in my store. He was robbing me blind while I was just outside! Here, see for yourself," said Shady, handing Shadow the picture. "Shady, I'm not a professional photographer, but I know a fake picture when I see one." How does he know it's a fake?

◆ "Excuse me, young man," said Ms. Tittle, dumping a pile of small bills and change onto the counter, "could I trouble you for a $20 bill?" Ms. Tittle pulled out a stamped, addressed envelope, explaining it was her son's birthday and that she always sent him $20 on his birthday. The clerk happily handed her a twenty, which Ms. Tittle quickly stuffed into the envelope and dropped into her purse. "Oh, excuse me, ma'am," stammered the young clerk, "there's only $19 here." "I'm so sorry," apologized an embarrassed Ms. Tittle. "Here, take your money back," she said, handing him the addressed envelope while taking back her bills and change. "Please keep the envelope handy while I run out to the car. I'm sure I must have a dollar in change between the seats." Strangely, Ms. Tittle never returned. Why not?

◆ Dr. Prod was about to putt when the worst possible thing happened—his pager went off. Reluctantly, Prod answered the call, only to hear a hysterical Harry Stable on the other end. "Dr. Prod, you've got to come quickly, Jane's had a terrible accident!" Dr. Prod had known Jane for years and he knew from Harry's tone of voice this was catastrophic. Prod dropped his putter and raced to his car. Twenty minutes later, Dr. Prod was at Jane's side, giving her an injection to ease the pain. An hour later Jane gave birth to her new baby. Less than 10 minutes later, Dr. Prod approached Harry to break the news every doctor dreads. The baby was fine, but the second injection Mary received proved to be fatal. Why would Dr. Prod have bothered giving Jane a second injection?

◆ Antonio Andretti looked up at the thousands of fans gathered for one of the biggest sports events of the season. Although he'd often imagined himself roaring around the end boards and down the straightaway to the checkered flag, in truth he had never driven in a major car race. Antonio gulped a glass of milk and waited for his cue. "Okay, you're on!" hollered one of the crew. Antonio could feel the vibration of the engine as it jumped to life. He sped out in front of the crowd, hoping beyond hope that they would follow his every turn. Deep in concentration, he soon forgot the crowd as he approached the first turn, well aware that a slip could send him crashing through the boards. For nearly a quarter of an hour he drove, always pushing his machine to the limit. In spite of his superb driving, the crowd paid little attention to his performance. Why not?

◆ Among the great cats, none has a more terrifying reputation than the tiger as a taker of human lives. Records over the centuries show a toll of thousands of deaths a year. One notorious killer, known as the Champawat Tigress, alone accounted for at least 436 victims. Unless threatened, tigers will almost always stalk and attack their prey from behind. Instead of trying to overpower and kill the tigers, in 1987 scientists took an about-face and invented a remarkably simple device to safeguard people entering the forests and

mangrove swamps of the Bay of Bengal region. What simple harmless device could possibly protect an unarmed human against these ferocious killers?

◆ Detective Shadow picked up the *Begile Beaver* and a black coffee and sat back at his desk. Beyond his window was a beautiful view of the Begile harbor. As dawn broke, he could see the cranes beginning to load the 20,000-ton Suijutsu freighter. Coincidentally, there was a front-page story about a Singaporean company that had purchased 40,000 Begile lawn tractors that were allegedly being loaded onto the Suijutsu that day. Further into the *Beaver,* Shadow read about a Singapore drug cartel that was rapidly increasing its Begile trade. "The good and the bad," thought Shadow as he finished his coffee and headed off to the City Hall courthouse. Seven hours later, Shadow was back at his desk writing his reports when he saw the Suijutsu leaving the island, bound for Singapore. At that moment Shadow suspected something very fishy about the freighter. Why?

◆ Detective Shadow surveyed the scene at the Sam Slug Detective Agency while Sam Slug explained the recent events. "It's no secret that I hated Sid Shady. Ever since he shafted me on our business deal, I've said I'd kill him, but that was just talk. I wouldn't be dumb enough to broadcast it now, would I? Anyway, his wife hired me to find out if he was stealing money from her trust fund. When I caught him and threatened to inform the missus, he went crazy. Here, listen for yourself." Shadow heard a voice on the answering machine threaten to come over and end Sam's life. "I thought he was just bluffing, but the next thing I knew, there was glass and bullets flying everywhere! Instinctively, I dove to my drawer and got my gun. Fortunately, my aim was a little better than his." "I'm afraid your self-defense story won't hold much water," replied Shadow. Why not?

◆ Detective Shadow stepped over the police line to see Constable Bumlinger hunched over the body. "What do we got, Bumlinger?" questioned Shadow. "It's a fairly routine case of suicide," replied Bumlinger, as if explaining the obvious. "As anyone can see, we have the body, the suicide weapon, and a suicide note with a 24-carat reason. What else could you want?" Shadow picked up the suicide note, which read: *"Goodbye world. My doctor tells me that I have less than 5 years to live, and the gold deposits that I discovered in the Begile*

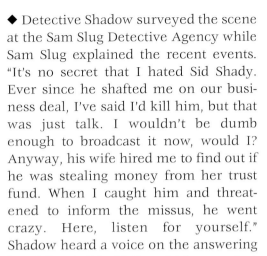

rain forest are apparently false. I've now lost my reason to go on. —H. L. Harry" Shadow checked H. L.'s wallet and found his I.D. but no money. He then stepped back and surveyed the scene for several minutes and said, "Bumlinger, even for you, it should be glaringly obvious that this man was murdered!" How does Shadow know?

◆ Constable Bumlinger snatched the note from Beulah Bile's shaking hand and read:

"I've got Muffy. If you want your dog back you will be at the east phone booth at the Begile Central Park at 5:30 P.M.— ALONE. Make sure you bring the flawless 25-carat diamond tennis bracelet. When the phone rings, answer it and you will be given further instructions."

"What am I to do?!" shrieked Beulah. "Don't worry!" snapped Bumlinger. "We'll surround that park with under-cover cops and tail that bum to the end

of the Isle." At 5:30 a frightened Beulah answered the phone. The voice instructed her to give the diamond bracelet to Fat Joe, who would be sitting on the bench next to the phone booth. Beulah gave Fat Joe the bracelet as instructed. Surprisingly, Fat Joe took off out of the park so fast that nobody had a chance to tail him. How could he lose them so quickly?

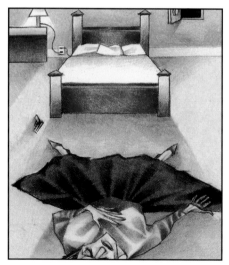

◆ "I ain't no murderer!" protested Sam Sham. "Old Lady Pringle's got more dia-monds than an African mine, so I came to take a few. I scaled up the vines growing on the side of the house, and the first window I looked into was the jackpot. The Pringles were yelling back and forth, really going toe to toe. Ms. Pringle was opening the safe, when she suddenly had a point to make. Next thing I knew, they took their fight downstairs. I climbed in and was help-ing myself when I heard them coming back. I dove under the bed when she came in followed by her husband. Then to my horror, I saw him pull a gun out of his smoking jacket and shoot her right between the eyes. He then dropped the gun and walked out. I waited until the coast was clear, then ran down the stairs to go out the front door, and that's when I ran into you." "Sorry, Sam," said Shadow, "but I ain't buying it." Why not?

◆ Sid Shady answered the pounding at his door and in barged Sam Slug with a duffel bag stuffed with cash. "I just knocked off Begile Bank. The cops are swarming all over! You gotta hide me!" Sid took one look at the cash and suddenly had an idea. "Sam, we gotta fake your death; it'll pull the cops off your trail. Start writing a suicide note while I figure how we'll stage it." Sam began writing furiously while Sid calmly put on a pair of gloves and loaded his .38. As soon as Sam finished writing, Sid pumped a shot into the side of his head. Sid dropped the gun at Sam's side and removed his gloves just as Shadow kicked Sid's door in. "Hey, Shadow," protested Sid, "I had nothin' to do with this. Here's all the money Sam robbed. He killed himself. Here, read the note!" Shadow took the note and then took Shady to headquarters for questioning. The next day Sid was charged with murder. How was he caught?

◆ Sam Sham passionately hated his wife, Candy, but he stuck around 'cause she had money, and plenty of it. Besides, Sam knew it wasn't wise to bite the hand that feeds you . . . unless you get caught. Sam thought long and hard about Candy's "accidental" demise until suddenly he had a plan: a slow, carefully administered poisoning. Although Sam would readily admit he was no chemist, he did own a chemistry set, somewhere, and he had taken high school chemistry. That night Sam brought Candy her favorite drink, pink

lemonade, just the way she liked it, with his own poisonous ingredients added: a highly reactive white metal mixed with chlorine gas. Sam happily watched Candy finish her drink and ask for three more. The only thing Sam observed was Candy getting giddy! Why didn't these deadly ingredients have any effect on her?

◆ Bartholomew Chassenée was a famous lawyer who practiced his profession in France during the 1500s. He made his bones by skillfully defending the poor, the homeless, and other unfortunates who couldn't afford the fees. In one famous trial in 1521, his client was accused of ravaging and terrorizing a local village. Chassenée successfully delayed the trial for more than a week when the court refused to grant his client the right to be judged by a jury of his peers. Chassenée's argument was that his client's rights were being violated, and that therefore the trial was essentially invalid. Why wouldn't the court have simply appointed a jury of the defendant's peers instead of wasting a week arguing the fact?

◆ On the left is a flock of Canada geese which always fly in a V-formation. Another constant in their flight pattern is that one leg of the 'V' is always longer than the other. A third constant is the apparent periodic confusion in their ranks when the birds change positions. Wind-tunnel tests have shown that this V-formation allows the geese to draft off each other, consequently allowing them to fly 70% further. The cause of their apparent confusion is that the lead goose grows tired of breaking the head wind, so they all take turns at the front in order to rest their leader. As in the picture on the left, why would one leg of the V-formation always be longer than the other?

♦ "This war, this confrontation which has been building for years," reported C. Shefield of CNN, "is finally over. From the beginning there were few rules, and neither side took prisoners. Any forces unfortunate enough to be caught were wiped out immediately. It was literally one against a thousand, and, incredibly, the larger forces lost! What was thought to be their strength was ultimately their weakness. Although they fought with machinelike precision, incapable of fatigue, their weakness lay in a total void of heart and emotion. Outmaneuvered by options of a billion to one, the smaller forces used cunning, creativity, and imagination to prevail." In what battle situation could forces so badly outnumbered be victorious?

♦ "I would like to propose a toast to my favorite daughter on her 30th birthday," said Suzie's father. "To say that rearing Suzie and her two brothers was a handful would be a colossal understatement. But then again," continued her father, "with Suzie being the oldest, it's only natural that all the trying moments of childrearing were experienced with her first. I'll never forget the time when Suzie didn't show up until 5:00 o'clock in the morning. By that time, her mother and I were so frantic I think we must have awakened the neighbors for miles around. The dogs were barking, the roosters were crowing, and I was fit to be tied." "Oh, pipe down, Dad," interjected Suzie. "It only happened once, and besides, it wouldn't have been possible for me to pull that stunt again even if I had wanted to." Why not?

◆ Dr. Prod's receptionist nodded to Mary and her daughter that they could go right in. "Hello, Mary," Dr. Prod said. "You're looking a little pale. Do you have a fever?" "Actually, Doctor, my daughter Nancy and I are both feeling the effects of a flu." Dr. Prod looked in Nancy's ear and under her tongue, and then took her temperature. He then gave Mary a similar examination and filled out a prescription for each of them. As they were leaving, Dr. Prod said, "Oh, by the way, Mary, on your way out please have my receptionist phone downstairs to the pharmacy to get your prescription ready." Just as Mary and Nancy were leaving the waiting room, they heard Dr. Prod's receptionist say to one of the patients, "That little girl just leaving is my daughter." How was this possible?

◆ Shawnassee the gardener is known for his green thumb. In fact, he likes the color green so much, he makes certain his garden is always green. Along with his green garden, he has green flowerpots, a green car, a green dog (dyed), a green lawn mower, and naturally, a green lawn. With all this being the case, what color would his greenhouse be?

◆ The moment Tung Chee-wa pulled his car up to the curb, Samson Wu ran out of his house in eager anticipation. "We had better hurry," Samson noted, looking at his watch, "The Beijing Jockey Club is 20 minutes away, and the tests begin in just 25 minutes." "How long did you study last night?" inquired Tung. "Last night?!" exclaimed Samson. "I've been cramming every night for the past 2 weeks. Honestly, Tung," admonished Samson, "if you expect to get a respectable score in this intelligence test and win a decent cash prize, you had better be prepared to study much harder or you'll be at the mercy of fate." What type of intelligence test were Tung and Samson taking?

◆ In 1936, Jane Chester, a teenager from Washington, Pennsylvania, quit her dishwashing job and headed to Hollywood in search of fame and fortune. Incredibly, she managed to appear in over 1,700 films produced by Columbia Pictures, but even more incredible was that fame and fortune eluded her all her life. She never received one cent from all her appearances. Why not?

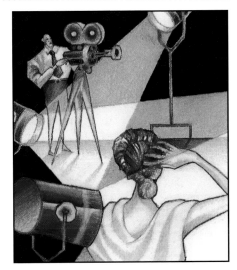

◆ It was Thanksgiving weekend in New York state, and school had just let out for 6 straight days. On instinct, Oliver and a few of his friends decided to go south for the winter. Although neither Oliver nor his friends had a vehicle, money, or travel plans, they managed to arrive in the sunny South without incident. Once there, they just hung out at the beach, ate, and drank and enjoyed the warm weather. They had such a good time, in fact, that none of them bothered returning to New York until spring. How did they manage to travel south and stay all winter without any money?

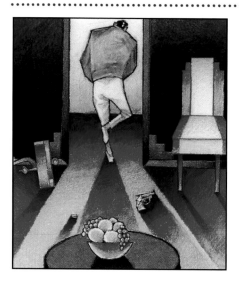

◆ It happened in Miami, in June 1996, that a man with a previous criminal record broke into an apartment to steal a gun. While he was there, the gun accidentally went off. Panicking, the burglar dropped the gun and fled the building. Although the thief had worn gloves and no one had seen him, when the police arrived they knew who the burglar was in a matter of minutes. How could they know?

◆ When World War I had just started, many of the fighting men wore only cloth caps. As the number of head injuries rose alarmingly high, metal helmets eventually replaced the cloth hats. Ironically, after issuing metal helmets, the number of head injuries was even higher. Since the fighting intensity remained constant, how can this strange phenomenon be explained?

◆ Willy Hope placed the Do Not Disturb sign on the handle and closed the door. Willy noted the time as 1:00 A.M. and called the front desk for a wake-up call at 11:00 A.M. Exhausted, Willy fell into bed and tried in vain to fall asleep. By 3:00 A.M., unable to sleep, Willy asked the front desk to page Sally, his business associate in the next room, with an urgent message. Luckily, Willy heard the phone ringing in Sally's room, and a few moments later he mercifully fell asleep. What could the ringing phone in Sally's room have had to do with Willy's ability to fall asleep?

◆ Art Bragg, the master of ceremonies, paced back and forth as he anxiously waited for Cardinal Bird's arrival. Unable to contain himself any longer, he walked to the podium and addressed the crowd on the most important subject he could think of—himself. "It seems only yesterday that I met the Cardinal when he first entered the priesthood . . . ," began Art. Mercifully, the Cardinal arrived several minutes later and forced Art to cut short his rambling autobiography and introduce the Cardinal. As the Cardinal addressed the crowd, he recalled that it was at this very town 30 years ago that he had heard his first confession, and that it was clearly the most disturbing because it involved a confession of murder. As the Cardinal finished his speech, a woman walked to the platform, pulled out a handgun, and committed murder. Whom did she kill, and why?

◆ Clem Walton was born an only child; he never married and seldom associated with anyone. Although Clem was a wealthy landowner, his true love was his stamp collection, reputedly worth a sizeable fortune. Shadow heard that Clem was ill, and when he knocked on Clem's door, he was shocked to be greeted by a lady. "I know you're shocked," she replied, "but so was I. I'm a nurse at St. Mary's, and when Uncle Clem called and said that he had fallen and injured his hip, I had to find his records. It was then I realized that he was my long lost uncle. I've taken a leave of absence from work until Uncle Clem is back on his feet. Why, I just finished helping him catalog his latest stamp, you know, the famous Monaco stamp depicting Franklin Roosevelt with six fingers on his left hand?" "I want to see Clem right now. You're an obvious fraud," said Shadow. Why?

◆ Ben Jonson, an English playwright and poet in 17th century England, once wrote, "Our whole life is like a play." It seems this metaphor had universal implications for Jonson. He died in 1637, and because of his friendly relations with King Charles I of England, he was buried in a sitting position. Why?

◆ Professor Beaker was the shipwreck's lone survivor. Stranded on a desert island and dying of thirst, Beaker luckily found a little pocket of fresh water on the pebbled shore which had pooled in a rock. Unfortunately, the only thing he had salvaged from the ship was a spoon, which was of little use in scooping out the water. Since the crevice was too narrow to make a ladle out of the spoon, how did Beaker manage to spoon the water out?

◆ Nobody knows exactly how it happened, but Gloria Goody got stranded on the island. Pictured right is her knight in shining armor, Barney Dribble. Unfortunately, Barney can't swim and neither can Gloria. The pond on which the island sits is 600 feet (960 km) in diameter and 30 feet (48 km) deep. Since Barney just happens to have 650 feet (1,040 km) of rope, exactly how can he rescue his fair maiden—Gloria?

◆ A passion for soccer is one thing most Europeans have in common. To attend a game is perhaps the most exciting of all. Soccer fans can overindulge in the electrifying atmosphere and the accompanying sights, sounds, and intensity of the crowd screaming for their favorite teams and players. Not long ago, Coventry, England, hosted a soccer tournament which drew the usual number of participants in the form of teams and fans. Following the introduction of the players and the singing of the national anthem, an announcement came over the P.A. asking the crowd to keep the noise to a minimum throughout the game. Why would such a strange request be made?

◆ Pictured on the left is a bottle of pear brandy. That by itself isn't overly intriguing, until one notices that there is a rather large pear inside the bottle and that the pear is at least twice the size of the bottle's opening. Two additional points of interest are that this is a perfectly normal pear and the bottle is a perfectly solid bottle with no breaks or patches. In fact, this bottle was chosen off the store's shelves where many others just like it were displayed. So, how did the brandy bottlers get the pear inside the bottle?

◆ Detective Shadow pushed the button of Begile Gem & Jewel and waited until the lock buzzed open. Shadow entered to find Sam Slug screaming at Art Conn that this was going to wipe him out. Art held a bloodied towel to his head, trying to dam the flow from the huge gash. "What happened?" inquired Shadow. A sheepish-looking Art Conn said, "Just as Sam stepped out for lunch, a young couple buzzed the door. When I let them in, the woman rushed at me holding a gun while her partner smashed the glass displays and took the jewelry.

Next thing I knew, Sam was screaming at me and calling the cops. I feel like I got hit by a truck." "What did they look like?" inquired Shadow. "That's just it," hollered Sam. "He doesn't know! He says they were wearing ski masks!" "I'm going to have to take you in for further questioning," said Shadow. Who does he take in and why?

♦ It was the first day of summer and it promised to be infinitely more pleasant than the last one, thought Beth, as she recalled the painful event of giving birth to her first daughter. Since her husband had the children for the day, Beth decided to take one-year-old Natalie on a picnic. Beth packed a lunch, a blanket, and some toys and headed to the park across the street. Beth spread the blanket and watched Natalie play in the grass with her toys while she soaked up the sun. Within moments, Beth had fallen asleep, only to wake several minutes later to see a large pit bull running towards Natalie. When the big dog reached Natalie he began to sniff and paw at her legs. Beth yelled at the dog to get lost, and when it took no notice, as dogs are wont to do, she decided to ignore it. Why would Beth have such a cavalier attitude?

♦ When Art Conn walked into the Soul-Ace Hotel carrying a small dog, Barney Dribble piped up, "Sorry pal, no dogs allowed." "This happens to be an Alsatian Padigo, one of the rarest breeds in the world," said Art. "I'm in the dining room negotiating a breeding contract. Watch him for a half hour and I'll give ya $20." As soon as Art left, Sam Sham entered the bar and exclaimed, "Where the heck did you get *that* dog!?" "He's not mine," replied Barney. "I'll give ya $500 for him right now," offered Sam. "No can do," replied Barney. "Look," said Sam, "I'll be back in an hour with $1,000. Give me that dog and it's all yours." Moments later a dejected Art Conn returned and said he couldn't pay Barney the $20 since the deal fell through. "Forget it," said Barney. "Say, if you need cash, I'll give you $300 for your dog." Art hemmed and hawed before settling for $500. How much money is Barney likely to make?

◆ When Louise first joined the West German police department, she was confronted with a resistance she couldn't have anticipated. Many of the officers had voiced their concerns that hiring her was taking the politically correct Equal Opportunity Employment Act too far. After all, she had been in an accident that had left her face slightly disfigured. When the town kids saw Louise they would taunt her by screaming, "Pig, pig, pig!" Louise bore it all in silent dignity. She remained on the staff because of her uncanny ability to sniff out the most concealed crimes. In spite of the continuous ridicule, Louise managed to rise above the taunts and go about her business. How could she manage to remain so cool and indifferent?

◆ Sid Shady slipped into the back row of the theater and strained his eyes to locate Sam Sham. Slowly, the image of Sam sitting 20 rows ahead came into focus. As soon as his eyes had adjusted, Sid pulled out his gun and methodically loaded 3 chambers. Sid didn't have anything against Sam personally, but everyone had to earn a living and Sid just happened to be a hit man. Besides, the pay was good and the hours were few. During a particularly quiet scene when the loudest sound was crunching popcorn, Sid fired 3 shots into the back

of Sam's head. Sid put his gun under his coat and calmly left the theater. It wasn't until the movie had ended that Sam's dead body was discovered. An autopsy confirmed that Sam had been shot 3 times and had died almost instantly. Since Sid didn't use a silencer, how could he have left the theater unnoticed?

◆ "Now you listen to me!" yelled Art Bragg to Buck Star, the owner of the *Begile Beaver*'s football club, "I've been producing television sports for 20 years, and Rule #1 is this: If you wanna win, you gotta control the ball. In order to control the ball, you gotta have an offensive star who can put the points on the board. Sign a major quarterback, and I'll give you the deal. Otherwise, forget it." As Buck Starr got up to leave, Art yelled again, "Now remember, I don't care if you're talking basketball, soccer, or polo for that matter, the team that's on offense has control of the ball!" "Well, that's where you're wrong," replied Buck. What situation was Buck referring to?

◆ Old Clem and Clodhopper left the barn and headed for the unplowed fields. Clem was the plowman, Clodhopper the horse. Clem knew from years of experience that Clodhopper took 124 steps to go from one end of the field to the other—that is, with each step of Clodhopper's 4 legs counting as one step. Anyway, as these things go, Clodhopper had just finished the last row when he decided he'd had enough for this lifetime. Right there and then, and just like that, he keeled over—dead. Given the above, how many hoof-prints will old Clodhopper have left behind in the second last row he plowed?

◆ Bumlinger chuckled to himself from behind his daily tabloid. "Hey, listen, Shadow. It says here in the *Begile Beaver* that some guy owns a two-headed rooster." Shadow always did his best to block out the office distraction known as Constable Bumlinger. "Another one here says: 'B. J. Wickers dealt second perfect deal in bridge in the last year.' That's pretty incredible! All four players get all 13 cards of one suit; and it happened twice in one year. Oh, and here's another one. A lady in Wyoming was attacked by a marauding band of 40-pound (18.2 kg) rabbits who stole all her credit cards. She spent 2 weeks in recovery at the hospital." "I might believe a couple of those stories," said Shadow, "but one of them is too hard to swallow." Which story is that and why?

◆ Art Conn, the emcee and chief organizer of Doubtbee's Annual Art Auction, held up his hand to silence the nervous energy of the anxious crowd. "Today's auction," began Art, "will begin with some valuable and rare Abraham Lincoln memorabilia. These treasures will include transcripts of the famous Lincoln–Douglas debates; several smiling Lincoln photographs, including Lincoln with his generals, Lincoln and his cabinet signing the Emancipation Proclamation, and some newly discovered personal letters writ-

ten by Honest Abe himself." It was just then that Professor Quantum stood up and said, "Mr. Conn, you have more gall than a penny-stock promotor, for you and your merchandise, sir, are completely fradulent!" Why would Quantum say that?

◆ Barney Dribble, who sported a large, fresh bump on his forehead, was found lying with his back on the sidewalk in front of the jewelry store window. His feet wore the familiar, warm, damp bowling shoes. Near his head lay his bowling ball and bag. The ambulance attendants were reviving the unconscious Dribble when Detective Shadow arrived. Shadow questioned several eyewitnesses and then arrested Dribble as soon as he was coherent. Since Barney Dribble did not have a criminal record and had not confronted or spoken to anyone that day, why would Shadow arrest him?

◆ Dee Septor, world-famous magician, yelled out: "Hurry, hurry, step right up for the greatest show on earth! Right before your very eyes I will change some wood into various shapes. Yes indeed, folks, you will not be disappointed. I have spent over 15 years perfecting this trick. I will begin by showing you some wood that I will shape into a perfect cube, and then, before your very eyes, I will change the same wood into the shape of a pyramid, and then into the shape of a cylinder. For the grand finale, I will transform this same wood back into the original cube!" How could Septor manage this feat?

◆ "Don't look surprised," Grandma Slug said. "It's true that I lost my hearing, but I can read lips, so ask me whatever you want." "Well," Shadow said, "I'd like to hear your account of your husband's death." "Well, it was a breezy day, like today, and Grandpa and I went out to the lake to sail. When dusk arrived, we anchored for the night. I was lying in the aft-cabin reading when Grandpa said he was going on deck for a spell. He always joked that most sailors died for the wrong reasons. Asleep on deck and an unexpected wave, and then, overboard." Just then the groundskeeper began the lawn mower, which caused Grandma to shout that they had better go inside. "As I was saying, when I went up on deck, his clothes were torn, and he was facedown in the water. Being deaf, I couldn't hear his cries for help." "You're lying to me, Grandma Slug," Shadow retorted. About what?

◆ It was that time of year when students were studying for their entrance exams for the next level of education. Professor Quantum was visiting several test-prep schools and found the treatment of the students astonishing. These elite students Quantum observed were all destined to be the doctors, engineers, and leaders of tomorrow. Incredibly, though, they were pampered beyond belief. Each afternoon, following the students' classes in chromatics, parallelism, and symmetry, they were actually given a

rest period. On several occasions, Professor Quantum witnessed teachers helping pupils with their lunch. Why would these intellectually gifted students be treated in such a delicate way?

◆ Delightful Trivia ◆

When zoologists examined a platypus for the first time, some scientists suspected a hoax. They thought that the parts of different animals had been sewn together. For more than 80 years after the first platypus skin arrived at the British Museum, scientists refused to believe in its existence.

In his younger days, French statesman George Clemenceau (1841–1929), popularly known as "The Tiger," fought a duel in a Parisian suburb. He bought a one-way ticket. "A one-way ticket?" said his secretary. "Are you pessimistic?" "Not at all," replied Clemenceau, "I always use my opponent's return ticket."

"How can you govern a country which has 246 varieties of cheese?"—Charles de Gaulle (1890–1970) of France

A concise book review: "The covers of this book are too far apart."—Ambrose Bierce (1842–1914)

"I didn't like the play, but then I saw it under adverse conditions—the curtain was up."—Groucho Marx (1895–1977)

"A portrait is a picture in which there is something wrong with the mouth."—Eugene Speicher (1883–1962)

"Major Strasser has been shot. Round up the usual suspects."—Julius J. Epstein, the movie *Casablanca* (1942)

"I didn't know he was dead, I thought he was British."—Anonymous

"Skill without imagination is craftsmanship and gives us many useful objects such as wickerwork picnic baskets. Imagination without skill gives us modern art."—Tom Stoppard (b. 1937)

"If we don't change direction soon, we'll end up where we're going."—Professor Irwin Corey

Last Will and Testament: "I owe much, I have nothing, and the rest I leave to the poor."—Francois Rabelais (1483–1553)

"A little inaccuracy sometimes saves tons of explanation."—Saki (1870–1916)

"You can lead a horse to water, but you can't make him float."—Anonymous

"Never give a party if you will be the most interesting person there."—Mickey Friedman

Lateral MindTrap® Puzzles

The Puzzle Answers

Answers for puzzles on pages 4–5

If Clem's musty old house had been boarded up for 7 years, the sterling silver cutlery would have been badly tarnished and not shiny. It was an obvious plant by the master of scams—Sam Sham.

When Shadow crossed the room to close the window, he noted the heavy candle drippings facing the window. With a steady breeze blowing through the window, the wax drippings would have formed on the opposite side. Shadow knew that Shady had tampered with the scene and had carelessly misplaced the candle.

Mike Peters was a 6-month-old baby.

Shady, who had the only key, said that neither he nor anyone else had been in the room for a week. If this was true, the leaves of the plant would have been leaning toward the window, not away from it.

Art Bragg would have suffocated in less than 2 minutes. By breathing through a 6-foot-long tube, he would be breathing the same air he expelled, rapidly reducing his oxygen level to zero.

It is impossible to maintain one's balance in this manner. As any gymnastics teacher would know, if your feet are in contact with a wall and you attempt to bend over without bending your knees, your center of gravity will no longer be over your feet, which will cause you to fall forward.

Dee Septor first makes certain that the surface area of the newsprint is smaller than the surface area of the cards. He then places the newsprint on top of the cards and releases the deck. They both fall to the ground at the same speed. (Try it!)

Dee was simply demonstrating a natural law of physics that states that all objects in freefall will accelerate at the same rate. We may consider this natural law to be false, since everyday situations seem to prove it doesn't appear to happen this way. Suppose we were to simultaneously drop a bowling ball and a sheet of newsprint from a height of 20 feet (6 m); we all know the bowling ball will hit the ground first. The reason—air resistance. By keeping the newsprint smaller than the cards, Dee has simply removed air resistance.

Professor Quantum flipped on the first switch and waited a couple of minutes. He then shut the first switch off, flipped on the second switch, and proceeded to go to the wine cellar. Once there, if the light was on, Quantum would obviously know that the second switch was the correct one. If it was still dark, Quantum would feel the lightbulb to see if it was warm. If so, the first switch was the correct one. If the bulb was both cold and dark, the correct switch would have to be the third one.

Sam and Sadie were actors in the play.

The passengers and crew were approaching the runway for takeoff when they were informed that the runways were closed and their flight was cancelled.

Barney was killed by the ice-cream peddler, Sam, who used a poisoned Popsicle.

The picture was of the three finalists in a beach beauty contest. The girl who was crying had just been crowned the winner and consequently was crying tears of joy. The two sad girls who were smiling were doing so because it was the proper thing to do.

Answers for puzzles on pages 10–11

Silicon Sally is a computer program.

In recent years, gangs of cyber terrorists have extorted between $400 and $800 million around the world. With a customized office management system costing as much as $125 million, financial houses in both New York and London have paid ransoms rather than have their computers crash. These orchestrated crashes are caused by information warfare devices such as high-emission radio-frequency guns, capable of blowing a devastating electronic storm through the system.

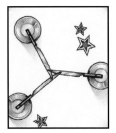

All bananas are picked while green, not yellow. Wild bananas in particular are both seedy and inedible. If a banana is picked when yellow, the starch will not turn to sugar, causing the banana to be tasteless. Further, should a banana be picked after it has ripened, the skin will usually break open, allowing bacteria to invade and cause it to rot.

As you can see, the trick is to make the 3 knives interlock while resting on the glasses.

Small house flies do not grow up to be big house flies; they're born full size, just like bees and butterflies. Larger flies are more likely to have been in the chrysalis longer and therefore are generally seen later in the year.

There couldn't be a grand staircase in a bungalow.

They were taken on the moon by Alan Shepard of Apollo 14. Since gravity on the moon has only one-sixth the pull of gravity on Earth, the ball travels considerably farther in the lighter atmosphere. Ed Mitchell, Shepard's fellow moonwalker, jokingly described the third shot as going for miles and miles (or kilometers and...).

There's no such language as Belgian. Languages spoken in Belgium include Dutch, French, Flemish, and Walloon.

He saw the lights of the cars below. Only two European countries drive on the left side of the road—Britain and Finland. Since it was a very large city he saw, and they were destined for Greece, Snorri knew it could only be London.

Although more than 50,000 pigeons were used as communications couriers in World War II, carrier or homing pigeons are strictly one-way birds. A pigeon is not able to take a message anywhere and then return home with an answer. The pigeon is taken along until a message needs to be sent back to the base—in this case, the bird's home. The message is then attached to the pigeon and it's released.

Dr. Probe simply replaced the hamster.

They were touring the Fresh Kills Land Fill (garbage dump) on Staten Island in New York State.

Porcupines cannot shoot their quills, since they lack the necessary muscular mechanism to fire them. A porcupine defends itself by raising its barbed quills and thrashing its tail to drive them into an attacker.

The barber was a woman.

She couldn't. She was a pig. This trial, and many others like it, actually took place in France in 1547. The accused were a sow and her piglets, who had killed and eaten a little girl. During the Middle Ages in France, pigs often freely roamed the village streets, and on rare occasions were known to attack and kill small children.

Everyone was sick—seasick. Lunch was aboard a cruise ship during a tropical storm.

Since the Bible wasn't written in Braille, Shady was obviously lying. Shady claims to have been reading when the commotion started, and then claims that he ran to the door and across the hall, etc. However, Shadow had to grope for the light switch when he entered Shady's darkened room.

Answers for puzzles on pages 18–19

They never lived to talk about it—they were all dead. When the ship was frozen in during the winter of 1762, without supplies, the entire crew died. Slowly the ship loosened herself from the ice and crept eastward year by year for 13 years, until a whaling vessel sighted it off the coast of Greenland on August 12, 1775.

Shadow knew that Shady was just testing security and that he didn't have the original painting. The real *Mona Lisa* is painted on a panel of wood and cannot be rolled or bent.

Harpo laid four quarters on the counter.

Dee Septor placed a hat on his head.

Hospitals never use feathered pillows since many people are allergic to them. Bumlinger swore that nothing had been brought in or out of the room. However, the murder weapon, the pillow, would have been rather difficult to get past an alert police guard.

Art had just caught a record-breaking fish, and, unable to wait any longer, he just had to call home and brag about his catch. In a fit of animation to demonstrate the size of his fish, Art accidentally put his hands through the windows and slit his wrists.

Barney. If Sam's statement is true, it would mean that Barney's and Art's statements are also true, which cannot be. Therefore, we know that Sam's statement is false. If Sid's statement is true, that would also mean that Barney's statement is true, which, again, cannot be. Therefore, Sam, Barney, and Sid have all lied, and Art's statement about his own innocence is correct. Since Barney's statement claimed his innocence, and we know that he lied, that means Barney is guilty.

Quantum was returning a library book that was $27.50 overdue!

If Barney had been the last person driving the little sportster as they had both maintained, it wouldn't have been possible for Bertha, being nearly 2 feet taller, to have jumped behind the wheel without some major seat adjustments.

If Sir Arthur's bicycle pump had been stolen as he claimed, he wouldn't have been able to inflate his tire.

Herring should have known that the letter addressed to Queen Elizabeth I was a fake. Queen Elizabeth I was not given a number until there was a second Queen Elizabeth. Beyond that, King George I could neither speak nor write the English language. Modern English, not Old English, was spoken in during his reign. The German-born prince communicated with his cabinet in French.

He exploded. Dan's friend was an astronaut in space. On Earth, air pressure pushes against the outside of the human body, which balances the pressures exerted from within the body. In space, where there is no external air pressure, a human being suddenly exposed to a perfect vacuum would explode.

Answers for puzzles on pages 24–25

The engine and fuel tank were the pilot himself, 26-year-old Bryan Allen. The airplane was the 70-pound (31.5 kg) Gossamer Albatross. The pilot pedaled the plane 23 miles (36.8 km) across the English Channel from England to France in just under 3 hours in June 1979. The Albatross, sheathed in a mylar skin less than 1,000 of an inch (0.01 mm) thick, had a 96-foot wing span. It was capable of cruising at 11 m.p.h. (17.6 km.p.h.) and required one-quarter horsepower to remain airborne. Fortunately, the pilot managed to exert one-third horsepower.

Sam overlooked two things. A rope that snaps while under tension will never have a clean cut, but rather, its ends will be frayed. Secondly, Mrs. Sham's body is on top of the rope, a rather impossible situation since she was supposedly hanging from the rope before it snapped.

The service was for his own beheading. Those condemned to die by the axe in Medieval and Renaissance England were strongly urged to tip the executioner to ensure he would do the job in one whack.

Josephine was a monkey. Murder can only be charged in the unlawful killing of a human being.

Sid Shady knew that payday meant people would be cashing their checks. Sid had poisoned the glue on several of the bank's deposit envelopes.

The battle was not trench warfare among men, but rather war between army ants of the Amazon jungle. In warfare these ants are known to act very much like humans. They are capable of deploying chemical sprays, taking slave labor, and of course, enjoying the spoils of war that go to the victor.

He needed a needle and thread to sew the Duke's head onto his body. The Duke of Monmouth had recently been beheaded for his involvement in an uprising against King James II. After his execution, it was decided to have his portrait painted for posterity.

William Congreve had been dead for 2 years. Henrietta became so deranged with grief at his death that she had a death mask made of Congreve's face and attached it to a life-size dummy. She insisted that guests and servants alike treat the dummy as if it were alive. She even went to the extent of having doctors examine the dummy whenever it became "ill."

Answers for puzzles on pages 28–29

The bingo hall was on the side of a hill. Beulah preferred to walk 660 feet (200 meters) downhill to the hall rather than 330 feet (100 meters) uphill.

Shadow's latest call was more urgent than giving Shady a ticket for double parking. Sam Sham's barging to the front of the line to use the instant teller was just Sam's "being himself."

The little prop plane was waiting to taxi and had not yet left the ground.

Barney had just been trapped for speeding. Having lost all his demerit points and wanting to avoid losing his license, he ran away from his car to report it as stolen. Barney knew that if he were caught again, he would lose his license—and, if unable to drive, his job, too.

July 4th occurs during the period of the longest days and shortest nights of the year. In northern Alaska, there is hardly any darkness at all. It would be pointless to try to view fireworks in a bright sky and nearly impossible to see any stars.

Dan was shot in the right temple. The objects on the desk, as well as their proximity, all indicate that Dan was very much a left-handed person. That being the case, Shadow could not believe that Dan would have used his right hand for something as monumental as ending his life.

The buyers explained that they too possessed a black tulip, and had destroyed this one in order to protect the uniqueness of their own.

Tulip speculation, like all bubbles, eventually burst, which incredibly brought the economy of Holland to a crashing halt. When the prices eventually cracked, many great families were ruined, old merchant firms were wiped out, and commercial life in Holland took years to recover from the disastrous speculation.

Despite their frequent appearance in major Renaissance paintings, oranges were not eaten at the Last Supper, simply because they were not introduced to the Holy Land until several hundred years after the Crucifixion. Returning Crusaders who reported seeing oranges in the Holy Land undoubtedly influenced Tintoretto and others.

Sir Henry Wyatt was kept alive by a cat. As legend has it, a cat wandered into his cell and took a liking to him. On occasion the cat would kill a pigeon and bring it to Wyatt, enabling him to stay alive. Eventually, when news of this miracle reached the king, he relented and ordered Wyatt released.

The car, which hasn't any exhaust pipes, is electric. It's unable to produce the poisonous gas—carbon monoxide.

If Sam had been at the beach all day as he claimed, he would not have been able to unlock his car and sit on the seats with a swimsuit and bare skin without getting badly burned.

It was the elderly lady. If she had really thought it was her room, she wouldn't have knocked before entering.

Answers for puzzles on pages 34–35

It's next to impossible for the scenario to have unfolded as Sam Slug explains. Barney could not have been holding a small revolver while wearing mittens. Even if that were possible, he couldn't have been holding both cases and the gun all at the same time.

Dan Manley was a volunteer fire fighter who managed to save the company's office from total destruction.

In this case Dr. Prod was the patient.

Not that Sid Shady minded the result, but Sam's death was an honest accident. Sam died by what is called space-bullet trauma. Sid Shady had fired several shots into the air in his wild celebration of July 4th, and one of those bullets had resulted in a freak accident. It had landed smack dab in the middle of Sam's head.

Sid tied the gun to the helium balloons before popping a couple of slugs into Sam Sham. After that, it was a simple matter of letting the balloons and gun float off into the wild blue yonder.

Sam probably set his aquarium outside as one of his stage props. After all, if it was cold enough to freeze the aquarium, it would have been cold enough to freeze Sam's water pipes, which meant there wouldn't have been any running water for coffee.

After rounding up the cats, the Persians began lobbing them over the walls to their death. The horrified Egyptians couldn't allow their divine creatures to be so sacrilegiously hurled about, and immediately surrendered.

The killer was a bull. Mark O'Connor was participating in the San Fermines, also known as the Running of the Bulls.

Answers for puzzles on pages 38–39

Tony's aunt. So many male Mafia bosses have been jailed recently that women are becoming Mafia dons to fill the vacated positions.

She wasn't anywhere near the scene of the accident. She and Sam had left for work that morning in different cars. They had been talking on their car phones when the accident occurred.

Shady had forgotten his keys and was breaking into his own house. The figure he saw moving was his own—in a mirror.

The briefcase left the train after its owner. Since the train was heading west and Shadow saw the case 165 feet (50 meters) further west than the body, the briefcase had to have been thrown out after the man had left the train.

Shadow knows that this scene was staged and that Sam was put into the car already bleeding. If the accident had occurred naturally, it would have been impossible for blood to be all over the step-plate, since the door would have been closed and prevented it from going anywhere beyond the interior. Further, with an impact of this magnitude, the car's air bags should have been triggered.

He soaked the label off one of the bottles and inscribed his message by poking holes in the label. Then he stuffed the message into one of the bottles and partially filled the other with sand. Next, he securely tied the necks of the two bottles together and let them float out to sea. The weight of the sand bottle would keep the message bottle safely underwater so that it could not right itself, release its trapped air, and sink.

He drove a snowplow in Mauna Kea, Hawaii.

Mauna Kea is home to 10 of the world's most sophisticated telescopes and houses dormitories full of astronomers. Situated 2.4 miles (4 km) above the tropical beaches, it receives regular snowfalls during the winter. Since the day–night temperature swings can rapidly turn the snow to ice, it has to be cleared immediately to keep the roads open. The five snowplow drivers commute from 79° F (26° C) weather at sea level to whatever winter snowstorms they may encounter on the big mountain. When the plow was first requested, the mainland manufacturer thought it was a joke and never bothered filling the order.

The picture's a fake since Art is holding the polo stick in the wrong hand. No player is allowed to hold a stick with the left hand. Polo players must control their ponies with the left hand and hold the stick in the right hand.

If Shady took a flash picture in front of his store window at night, the dark window would have reflected the flash like a mirror. Seeing anything through the store window would be impossible.

She was a con artist who just bilked the clerk behind the counter. This old con is known as the envelope switch. When Ms. Tittle gave the young clerk an envelope, it merely contained newsprint, not the $20 bill she had just stuffed into another envelope.

The second injection was given to put her out of her misery. Jane was a pregnant racehorse with a broken leg.

Unfortunately for Antonio and his vivid imagination, he was merely driving a Zamboni (an ice-resurfacing machine) between periods of a hockey game.

It's a plastic face mask worn on the back of the head. Since tigers always attack from behind, a person with a face mask on the back of the head appears to have no back. Several thousand men who have worn these masks in the forest report that tigers have followed them, visibly confused—and have given up the hunt without bothering to attack.

Shadow noticed from reading the depth numbers on the side of the Suijutsu that it was riding at just about the same height as it had been in the morning. If 40,000 lawn tractors had just been loaded onto the freighter, it would be sitting considerably lower in the water than it had been in the morning, when empty.

All of the shattered glass is outside of Sam's office, which means that he obviously fired first. If Shady had fired first, as Sam maintains, the glass would have fallen inside.

There are two reasons Shadow knows H. L.'s corpse was placed there. First of all, there's an excessive amount of blood on his clothing and virtually nothing on the surrounding pavement. Second, and more telling, is the fact that inexplicably, the blood defies gravity—it's flowing out of the wound uphill.

Fat Joe was a homing pigeon. Beulah was instructed to take Fat Joe out of the cage, fasten the bracelet to his ankle, and release him. Since a trained homing pigeon can travel at speeds of 50 miles (80 km) per hour for distances of several hundred miles (km), it was impossible to track him.

Sam claimed that he dove under the Pringles' bed when they returned to the bedroom. Unfortunately for Sam, the Pringles owned a waterbed. A waterbed sits directly on the floor, which makes it impossible to dive under.

If Sam had killed himself, as the note alleges, Sam's fingerprints should have been on the gun, and gunpowder residue should have been detected on his hands. Since neither were found, there could be only one cause of Sam's death—Sid Shady.

When Sam's "deadly" mixture of a highly reactive white metal (sodium) and chlorine were combined, they produced one of the world's most common chemical compounds—table salt.

. . . .

Answers for puzzles on pages 48–49

. . . .

The accused was a bear, and a jury of his peers would naturally have been a group of bears.

In another famous trial, a group of rats was accused of destroying a barley crop. When the summons was issued and his clients failed to appear, Chassenée argued that his clients feared that the prosecution would discharge evilly disposed cats on them. Therefore, he demanded that the prosecution grant a cash guarantee ensuring the rats safety on their way to court. When the prosecution refused to post the cash, the case was dismissed. During the Middle Ages there were many legal trials involving animals, birds, and even insects.

There's more geese in it.

Okay, we admit it, that question was an obvious setup and not at all fair.

Note: Here's a second chance to gain a point. What is the difference between a gaggle of geese and a skein of geese?

A dictionary will provide the answer.

This war was the February 1996 chess challenge pitting Deep Blue and the IBM research team against Grand Master Gary Kasparov. Of the six matches, Deep Blue won the first, Kasparov the second. The third and fourth were draws, and Kasparov won the fifth and sixth.

Although Deep Blue is capable of examining a billion moves per second, ultimately it was Kasparov's human creativity which triumphed over the brute force of silicon.

Note: In May 1997, Deep Blue defeated Kasparov, marking the first time a computer had defeated a chess Grand Master.

It was the day Suzie was born.

Dr. Prod's receptionist is the husband of Mary and the father of the little girl, Nancy.

It would be clear!

They were going to the track to bet on the horse races. In China, gambling is a taboo pastime, so people visiting the Beijing Jockey Club take what's known as an "intelligence test." This test involves guessing about horses travelling around a track, with the most "intelligent guesses" receiving cash prizes.

She appeared as Columbia's Statue of Liberty. Jane was just one of many girls asked to pose. She recalls, "No one really knew if the picture would be used. We weren't paid, but we hoped it would lead to something."

They flew. Oliver and his friends were geese.

When the gun went off, the burglar had accidentally shot his thumb off. In his haste, he failed to take it with him.

Although the number of head injuries increased, the number of deaths declined significantly. Many soldiers who would have died wearing the cloth caps were now staying alive and surviving head injuries. A soldier killed from a head injury became a death statistic rather than a head-injury statistic.

Sally was snoring so loudly, Willy couldn't fall asleep. The ringing phone woke her up, enabling Willy to finally get some peace and quiet.

Art Bragg. Art Bragg had been crowing about being the first person the Cardinal had ever heard in a confession. The Cardinal later revealed that the first confession he'd heard was one involving murder. The woman had always suspected that it was Art Bragg who had murdered her husband, and today she had her proof.

Since Clem was an only child who had never married, it wouldn't have been possible for him to have a niece.

There was no more room. King Charles I had promised Ben Jonson that he could be buried anywhere he wanted in Westminster Abbey. Jonson chose his spot, and when he died it was discovered that someone else had beaten him to it. There was however an area about 18 × 18 inches (45 × 45 cm) that was available. Determined not to break a dead man's wish, the king's men employed a little ingenuity and Jonson was buried in a sitting position in an upright coffin.

Beaker began dropping the readily available pebbles into the hole until the water level rose enough for the spoon to be effective.

Barney ties one end of the rope to the tree and then walks all the way around the lake and back to the same tree. During Barney's travels, the rope naturally wraps itself around the island's tree. When Barney secures the other end of the rope to *his* tree, it is doubled and firmly stretches between both trees. At this point, it is quite safe for Barney to watch Gloria pull herself through the water by means of the taut rope.

The tournament was for five teams of blind soccer players. The soccer ball they used was filled with 100 ball bearings. Everyone had to remain quiet so the players could hear the ball's location.

The pear was grown inside the bottle. In the spring, just after the blossoms have turned into tiny pear buds, the farmers secure the empty bottles onto the trees using wire and string. Several months later, when the pears are large and ripe, the bottles are picked (with the pears inside of course) and cleaned and filled with pear brandy.

Art Conn. If the robbers were wearing ski masks, as Art maintains, Art was either involved in the robbery or was incredibly stupid to have let them in. The store's security system, which includes a front-door camera and monitor, is there so that anyone looking suspicious will be let in.

The pit bull wasn't really hurting Natalie and besides, Natalie, a Doberman pinscher, was large enough to take care of herself.

Nothing! Barney Dribble was the marked boob in this old swindle between Art Conn and Sam Sham. There's no such breed as an Alsatian Padigo, and Barney has just become the proud owner of a $500 mongrel.

Louise didn't mind being called a pig because she was one. Louise was a 230-pound (103.5-kg) pig.

Pigs, used for finding buried truffles, can sniff to a depth of 4½ feet (1.3 m) underground. Furthermore, Louise's trainer maintained that she couldn't be put off the trail by other smells, noises, or abstractions like canines could. The resistance to Louise's employment both from the officers on staff and from the Interior Ministry of Lower Saxony was based on the fear that a pig on staff would tarnish their image. A huge argument ensued that was eventually won by the pig lovers and Louise remained employed. She earned about $50 per month, which allowed her to pig out on her favorite type of food—pastries.

Sid Shady shot Sam Sham with a blowgun using poisoned darts.

Blowguns, which have been used in many cultures and societies throughout history, are not only silent but extremely powerful and accurate. A 3-inch (7.5 cm) cone dart's initial muzzle velocity is approximately 300–400 feet (90–120 m) per second, and a dart is capable of being blown with enough force to penetrate ¼-inch (0.6-cm) pegboard.

Baseball. In baseball, it's the defense that controls the ball.

None. The plow overturns the soil and covers any hoofprints left by the horse.

Shadow couldn't believe the perfect deal. Every once in a while, a local bridge club or newspaper will report that a perfect deal has occurred—with all four players receiving a complete suit. However, it's almost certain that these reports are false.

A perfect deal is so unlikely (the odds against it are 2,235,197,406,895,366,368,301,560,000 to 1) that some think it has probably never happened in the history of bridge. If someone in the world were dealt 120 bridge hands a day, a perfect deal would occur only once in 62 trillion years.

There are no photographs of Abraham Lincoln smiling.

In old photographs dating from the late 1800s through the early 1900s, people rarely smiled. In the early days of photography, exposure times were much longer than they are today, and holding a smile for such a long time would not only be uncomfortable, but it would also look phony. Photographs were considered serious business. To have a photographic portrait was a relatively rare experience, and when it happened, subjects tried their best to imitate the subjects of portrait painters.

Answers for puzzles on pages 62–63

Barney Dribble had thrown his bowling ball at the jewelry store window in an attempt to grab the jewels and run. Much to Barney's surprise, the window was made of a special tempered glass. When Barney threw the ball at the window, it bounced back, hit him on the head, and knocked him unconscious.

Much to the furious disbelief of the audience, Dee Septor simply had a box of sawdust, which he poured into the hollow cube, and then into the container shaped like a pyramid, and then into the cylinder, and, finally, back into the cube shape.

If Grandma Slug was as deaf as she claimed, she would not have known to raise her voice above the sound of the unseen lawn mower.

They were very young Japanese children who were preparing for entrance into elite kindergartens.

Over 150 such schools are in the Tokyo area that coach preschoolers to ace entrance exams for fast-track kindergartens. The chances are 10 to 1 in getting a placement. Among the lessons are knowing colors, shapes, and nursery rhymes.

Also children were taught: Don't cry or whine. Sit with your hands politely resting on your thighs. Never take more than one cookie when offered the cookie jar.